BREAD BAKING RECIPE BOOK FOR BEGINNERS

100+ Easy, Homemade Bread Recipes—
From No-Knead Classics to Artisan-Style
Loaves Anyone Can Make

by

Dana Albright

information does not mean that the author or the publisher endorses the information the organization or website may provide or recommendations it may make.

Please remember that Internet websites listed in this work may have changed or disappeared between when this work was written and when it is read.

Bread Baking Recipe Book for Beginners :
100+ Easy, Homemade Bread Recipes—From
No-Knead Classics to Artisan-Style Loaves
Anyone Can Make

Table of Contents

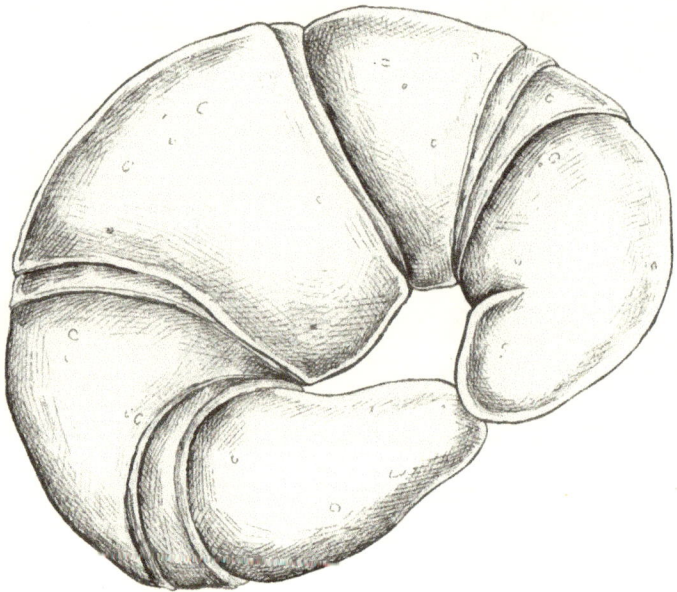

INTRODUCTION

B read has been a cornerstone of human nourishment for thousands of years, and its comforting aroma and satisfying texture have warmed countless kitchens across the world. For a novice baker, the idea of making bread at home might seem intimidating, but it's also incredibly rewarding. This book is designed to guide you through that process with clarity and encouragement, breaking down each step so you can build confidence right from the start. Whether you're aiming to bake a crusty artisan loaf or a soft sandwich bread, this is the place to begin your journey.

At its heart, baking bread is about transforming a handful of simple ingredients into something truly special. Flour, water, yeast, and salt come together in a fascinating dance of chemistry and craft, yielding bread that's not just food, but an experience. This guide doesn't just give you recipes — it helps you understand the why behind each step, so you'll know what to expect and how to troubleshoot if things don't go as planned. That understanding can turn baking from a mysterious process into a joyful, creative act.

Many beginners worry about needing fancy kitchen gadgets or specialized ingredients to bake good bread. Rest assured, the tools required are modest and often already found in your kitchen, or easily replaced with affordable alternatives. This book will help you find the right balance of tools that suit your needs without overwhelming you. You'll also discover techniques that don't demand long hours or complicated steps but produce delicious results every time. There's no need to be an expert to start; with some patience and guidance, anyone can enjoy fresh bread made at home.

One of the most exciting parts of bread baking is how it invites experimentation and personal flair. Once you're comfortable with foundational methods, you can tweak recipes, try different flours, or even explore naturally fermented sourdough breads. The chapters ahead will gently guide you through these possibilities, but all of that begins with building a strong base, which is exactly what we'll focus on here.

Expect to learn not only how to mix and knead dough, but also how to recognize subtle cues during fermentation, proofing, and baking that will help you judge when your bread is at its peak. This is valuable knowledge that transforms baking from mindless following of instructions into an intuitive craft. You'll start seeing the shifts in dough texture and rise that signal progress, giving you confidence to bake without rigid reliance on timers or thermometers.

It's important to remember baking bread is a skill nurtured over time. Not every loaf will turn out perfectly, and that's part of the process. Embracing mistakes as learning opportunities is how you'll improve—and find joy in the journey. This book encourages a patient, forgiving approach that lets you grow at your own pace. It's rewarding to see your hands shape dough into loaves that smell warmly inviting and taste delicious, a simple pleasure worth the effort.

Throughout this book, you'll find over 100 recipes crafted to suit various tastes and skill levels. From quick and simple breads you can whip up on a weeknight, to more involved doughs that reward time and attention, the collection has something for everyone. You'll also discover how to store and freeze bread properly so your homemade loaves last longer and retain their freshness. Learning these practical tips early will help keep your baking experience fun and sustainable.

Many who start baking bread seek a deeper connection to their food and the rituals that accompany making it from scratch. Bread is more than nourishment; it's a symbol of care shared around tables with family and friends. This book honors that tradition by weaving together practical advice and heartfelt encouragement. Whatever your reasons for baking—whether to save money, eat healthier, or simply enjoy the creative process—there's a place here for you.

Finally, this guide recognizes the diverse needs and preferences of home bakers. You'll find options for traditional yeasted breads as well as sourdough starters, enriched doughs like brioche, and gluten-free recipes. The goal is to inspire you to keep exploring different types of bread while building a solid understanding of the basics. Bread baking is an adventure worth embarking on, and with a bit of practice, your kitchen will be filled with the rewarding smells and tastes that only homemade bread can deliver.

Let's begin this exciting journey together, where flour-dusted hands and rising dough mark the start of your bread baking story. The chapters ahead will offer you straightforward recipes, clear explanations, and plenty of encouragement to help you master the art and science of baking bread right at home. Soon enough, the crusty, golden loaves you create will be proof of your growing skills and the delicious fruits of your efforts.

Chapter 1
Bread-Baking Foundations

———————————— ⟫⟫⟩ ⟨⟨⟨⟨ ————————————

Bread baking starts with understanding the basics that turn simple ingredients into something truly magical: flour, water, yeast, and salt. Each component plays a critical role—flour provides structure, yeast brings life through fermentation, water activates gluten and yeast, and salt enhances flavor and controls fermentation. Before diving into recipes, it's important to get familiar with the core techniques and tools that make the process approachable and enjoyable, from mixing methods to kneading styles and the art of shaping. Knowing why your dough behaves a certain way or what a recipe's timing means will save you frustration and empower you to solve problems confidently. This chapter sets the stage by grounding you in the essential knowledge and mindset needed to build your bread-baking skills, ensuring you feel ready to take on more complex loaves throughout the book.

Bread 101: How Bread Works

Bread is a beautiful balance of a few simple ingredients—flour, water, yeast, and salt—that come together to create something greater than the sum of their parts. When flour and water mingle, gluten forms, giving dough its structure and stretch, while yeast works behind the scenes, eating sugars and releasing carbon dioxide to make the dough rise and develop flavor. Salt not only seasons but also tightens gluten and controls yeast activity, ensuring your loaf has the right texture and taste. Understanding how these ingredients interact helps you predict how dough will behave as you mix, knead, and bake, turning basic components into the comforting, crusty breads that fill your kitchen with warmth. Mastering these fundamentals sets the stage for every recipe that follows, making bread baking more approachable and rewarding from the very first loaf.

The Science of Flour, Water, Yeast & Salt—these four ingredients form the heart of every bread recipe, yet their simple appearance masks the complex chemistry and biology that happens once they meet. Understanding how each one behaves and interacts not only helps you avoid common pitfalls but also inspires confidence to experiment and truly master bread baking from the very start. Let's break down the role each plays and why their balance matters so much in every loaf.

Flour is more than just a powdery base. It's the skeleton of your bread, supplying the proteins and starches necessary to structure the dough. When you add water, it activates these components. The proteins in the flour—mainly glutenin and gliadin—begin to bond and form gluten, a stretchy, elastic web that traps gas produced by yeast. This network is crucial because it's what gives bread its chew and allows the dough to rise. The amount of protein in your flour influences how strong and elastic your gluten network will be, which means that not all flours perform the same way in bread baking.

Next comes water, which might seem straightforward but plays multiple essential roles. It hydrates the flour, enabling gluten formation, and initiates enzymatic activity that breaks down starches into simpler sugars. These sugars fuel yeast, which in turn produces carbon dioxide gas and alcohol during fermentation. Water temperature also affects fermentation speed; warmer water encourages yeast to work faster, while cooler water slows it down, giving you more control over timing. Water's ratio to flour—the hydration level—has a profound impact on dough texture and crumb openness, so it's something you'll get to fine-tune as you experiment with recipes.

Yeast, the living organism that makes bread rise, brings its own special magic. It feeds on the sugars released from the flour's starches, converting them into carbon dioxide gas and alcohol through fermentation. The gas inflates the gluten network, causing the dough to expand and develop that airy structure we all yearn for. Yeast also contributes to flavor development, as fermentation produces a range of organic acids and compounds that enrich the taste and aroma of the bread. Whether you're using active dry yeast, instant yeast, or a natural sourdough starter, the science behind yeast remains fascinatingly similar.

Salt, although used sparingly, has an outsized impact on both flavor and dough performance. It tightens the gluten network, strengthening the dough and improving its elasticity and chew. Salt also regulates yeast activity, preventing fermentation from happening too quickly, which can help develop better crumb and taste. Moreover, salt enhances the overall flavor, balancing sweetness and masking bitterness that might develop during fermentation. Skipping salt or using too little disrupts this delicate balance, often resulting in bland or overly airy bread.

The interaction between these four ingredients really comes down to balance and timing. Flour and water need to hydrate thoroughly to form gluten, while yeast must be active enough to produce gas but not so aggressive that it exhausts itself before baking. Salt needs to be evenly mixed to reach every part of the dough without directly touching yeast, as it can inhibit its activity if it does. When these components work in harmony, the dough transforms from a simple mixture into a living entity, capable of rising, expanding, and developing complex flavors.

One of the more subtle but fascinating aspects is how the hydration level—a fancy term for the ratio of water to flour—affects not just texture, but also how easy or challenging the dough is to handle. Lower hydration doughs, with less water, tend to be stiffer and denser, resulting in a tighter crumb and a more traditional sandwich bread texture. Higher hydration doughs are wetter and stickier, often producing open, chewy crumb structures typical of artisan-style loaves like ciabatta or sourdough. As a home baker, you'll soon learn how adjusting hydration lets you customize your loaf's personality to match your taste and lifestyle.

Flour quality and type also feed into this science. Each kind of flour has different protein levels, enzymes, and mineral contents, which affect how water is absorbed and how gluten forms. While we'll dive deeper into selecting flours later in this chapter, it's worth noting here that the basic roles of flour remain consistent: it's the building block of gluten and starch. However, its source and processing can tip the balance, influencing everything from dough elasticity to crust color.

Yeast's activity is equally intricate. It's not just about microbes eating and producing gas—they respond to temperature, pH, and the availability of nutrients. Warmer temperatures speed up fermentation but risk exhausting yeast too quickly, leading to off-flavors. Cooler temperatures slow down the process, giving more time for complex flavor compounds to develop. You'll find that different bread styles and recipes call for tweaking these variables to achieve the ideal rise and taste.

Salt's regulating effect might surprise you if you're new to bread baking. Without salt, yeast can over-produce gas and cause the dough to rise uncontrollably fast. This rapid fermentation may sound good, but it actually results in weaker gluten structure and less flavorful bread overall. Salt tempers yeast's enthusiasm, ensuring a slower, steadier fermentation that allows the dough's texture and taste to mature fully.

When you mix flour, water, yeast, and salt, the resulting dough is a delicate, living system. Each ingredient affects the others, so small changes or mistakes can ripple through the process. For example, too little water reduces gluten formation and yeast activity, leading to a tight, dense loaf. Too much water can weaken the gluten, making the dough sticky and hard to shape. Using too much yeast speeds up fermentation but may give your bread a yeasty, sharp flavor that doesn't suit all palates. Without enough salt, your bread can taste flat and lack structure. Understanding these relationships helps you troubleshoot and refine your technique.

It's helpful to think of bread dough as a living ecosystem, where flour is the habitat, water is the weather, yeast are the inhabitants, and salt acts as a regulator maintaining balance. Each needs to be just right for the community to thrive and produce a loaf that's flavorful, fluffy, and beautifully textured. This perspective makes the science less intimidating and more intuitive, guiding how you mix, ferment, and bake.

Every loaf you bake will deepen your appreciation for how these components dance together. Sometimes a recipe might look simple on paper, but the way the ingredients respond to your kitchen environment, flour brand, or timing can change the outcome. This is where experience, patience, and a little curiosity become your best tools. The more you observe dough behavior—how it feels, looks, and smells—

you'll start to grasp this science in real time, eventually baking bread that delights you and anyone lucky enough to taste it.

Before we move on to flour selection and yeast types, keep this foundational understanding close: flour forms the structure, water activates it, yeast brings life, and salt shapes the process and flavor. Together, they make bread more than just food—they make it a rewarding craft you can master in your own kitchen. With each loaf, you'll learn more, bake with greater confidence, and enjoy the timeless satisfaction of turning these simple ingredients into something truly magical.

Choosing the Right Flour for Each Loaf is a crucial chapter in understanding how your bread will turn out, even before you start mixing ingredients. Flour isn't just flour—it comes in many varieties, each with its characteristics that influence texture, flavor, crumb structure, and rise. For a beginner, knowing which flour to choose for the loaf you're making can feel a bit overwhelming, but breaking it down into manageable parts makes it easier to decide.

First, think about what you want your bread to be. If you're aiming for a classic, soft sandwich bread, a flour with moderate protein content, like all-purpose flour, usually works perfectly. On the other hand, if you're after a chewier, more structured loaf such as a baguette or a hearty country bread, bread flour, which has higher protein, will give you that stronger gluten network necessary for that open crumb and good rise. The protein content in flour essentially determines how much gluten develops when mixed with water, and gluten is what provides elasticity and chew to your bread.

Many home bakers start with all-purpose flour because it's widely available and versatile. It's often sufficient for simpler breads and will yield tender, pleasant results in white loaves or softer rolls. However, if you want to experiment with rustic artisan breads, reaching for bread flour will improve your chances of success. The extra protein in bread flour bonds more firmly and traps gas from fermentation better, allowing your dough to spring up with volume and lightness. You may notice that breads made with all-purpose flour sometimes come out denser and less airy, especially if the recipe calls for long kneading or fermentation times.

Whole wheat flour deserves special attention here. Since it contains the entire wheat berry, including bran and germ, it brings more flavor, nutrition, and a denser crumb. However, bran particles actually cut through gluten strands, which weakens the dough's structure. So, when baking with whole wheat flour, you can expect your bread to be heavier unless you mix it with white or bread flour. A common beginner tip is to start with substituting no more than 25 to 30 percent whole wheat flour into your white flour recipes. This way, you get the wholesome, nutty taste and extra fiber without sacrificing too much rise or lightness.

For those drawn to darker, more robust breads like rye or pumpernickel, rye flour changes the game entirely. Rye contains different types of proteins called pentosans, which absorb water differently and don't develop gluten the way wheat proteins do. This means rye breads tend to be much denser and more compact, often requiring sourdough fermentation techniques or a blend with wheat flour to help the structure. Rye also imparts a distinctive earthy and slightly sour flavor profile that can be wonderful in sandwich loaves or artisan-style rounds but isn't suited to every kind of bread.

If you glance at most bread recipes, you'll notice how often they specify the type of flour. This is intentional because moisture absorption varies significantly between flour types. Bread flour, being higher in protein, soaks up more water, making dough stickier and more elastic. Whole grain flours, bran-heavy flours, or rye flours also require extra hydration to soften the dough and avoid dry, crumbly results. As a beginner, adjusting hydration when switching flours is one of the subtle skills you'll develop with practice—it's less about following strict measurements and more about feeling the dough and learning from experience.

Gluten development is tied closely to the flour you use. Not all recipes require the same level of gluten strength. For example, enriched breads like brioche or challah, with added fats and eggs, call for soft wheat flour or even pastry flour, offering tender crumbs because too much gluten can make the loaf tough. In contrast, rustic country loaves depend on a robust gluten network to hold gas bubbles, so bread flour or strong flour blends are preferred. Understanding this helps you tailor your flour choice to the end texture and flavor you want, even if you don't yet tweak individual protein percentages or enzyme activity.

Many flour packages will list protein content, typically ranging from 9% in cake flours up to 14% in strong bread flours. As a beginner, you can use this as a quick guide. A good rule of thumb is: 9-11% protein for tender, light breads and pastries, 11-13% for firm bread with some chew, and above 13% for really strong bread that needs maximum elasticity like baguettes or pizza dough. If you live somewhere that doesn't have labeled protein content, asking your local mill or reading product descriptions from online sellers can help you get a better picture.

Besides standard flours, whole-grain blends, ancient grains like spelt or einkorn, and specialty flours add complexity, but they usually require recipe adjustments and longer fermentation to develop flavor and crumb properly. You might want to try these once you're comfortable with basic flours because they often behave differently, sometimes hybridizing gluten in fascinating ways but challenging your dough's texture.

For beginners, one of the best approaches is to start with 100% bread flour or all-purpose flour for most recipes, then gradually incorporate whole wheat or rye flours as you learn how each affects dough behavior. Mixing flours allows you to experiment with both texture and taste without risking a loaf that's too dense or lacking flavor. The proportion you choose depends on the recipe's purpose; a hearty sandwich loaf might comfortably take 30% whole wheat, while a sourdough boule often benefits from a higher ratio of whole grain.

Another factor that affects how flour behaves is freshness. Flour that's been sitting for months might lose some of its baking power as natural enzymes degrade, making it less effective at gluten development and yeast feeding. Store your flour in a cool, dry place, ideally sealed, and consider rotating through your supply by buying smaller quantities so your bread-making always starts with the freshest, most active flour possible.

It's also worth mentioning that gluten-free flours play by completely different rules. They require different binding agents and hydration balances since the gluten network you rely on in wheat flours is absent. This section focuses on traditional wheat-based flours, but if you're interested in gluten-free baking, specialized recipes and blends will guide you there.

Finally, choosing the right flour isn't just about protein numbers and type. It's about developing a feel for what your dough needs. When you mix flour with water and yeast, you'll notice its texture, stickiness, and elasticity. This tactile feedback will guide you in adjusting hydration and mixing time. In time, you'll intuitively know that your bread flour is ready when the dough pulls away cleanly from your hands and feels springy—a clear sign that the gluten is developing well.

Bread baking is a delightful journey, and understanding flour choices sets the foundation for all the loaves to come.

With every batch, you'll gain confidence in selecting the right flour for each type of bread you want, whether it's a soft sandwich loaf, a crusty artisan boule, or a nutty, dense whole wheat creation. Start simple, experiment slowly, and enjoy the process of discovering what each flour can do for your bread.

Yeast vs. Sourdough Starter: When to Use Which
When you're first stepping into the world of bread baking, one of the biggest decisions you'll face is choosing between commercial yeast and a sourdough starter. Both are powerful leavening agents that bring bread to life, but they offer very different experiences, flavors, and processes. Understanding when to use yeast or sourdough starter will help you become more confident in your baking choices and tailor your loaves to suit your time, taste preference, and baking goals.

Commercial yeast, often labeled as instant or active dry yeast, is the reliable workhorse in many home kitchens. It's a cultivated strain of Saccharomyces cerevisiae that's available in a convenient, predictable form. If you want your dough to rise quickly and reliably every time, yeast is the go-to. It's a great choice for beginners because it simplifies the fermentation process—you mix, knead, proof, and bake within hours rather than days. Yeast kicks off fermentation, producing carbon dioxide rapidly, which puffs up your dough and creates the familiar airy crumb structure. Its flavor profile is typically mild and neutral, letting the bread's other ingredients shine through. This is especially true for enriched breads, sandwich loaves, and any recipe where you want a soft, tender crumb without tanginess.

On the other hand, a sourdough starter is a living culture made up of wild yeasts and various beneficial bacteria, especially lactobacilli. This culture develops over time through fermenting flour and water, drawing wild microbes from the environment into a symbiotic colony. Unlike commercial yeast, sourdough fermentation is a slower, more complex process. The wild yeasts provide a gentler rise, while the bacteria generate lactic and acetic acids, lending sourdough bread its signature tangy flavor and deeper aroma. It's a slower path to bread but one rich with character and nuance. If you're someone who enjoys a hands-on approach and is eager for bread with complex flavor layers and a chewy, crusty texture, sourdough will reward your patience.

Timing is a key factor when deciding which to use. If your schedule demands speed, commercial yeast is often the better option. You can mix dough in the morning and enjoy fresh bread by evening. Quick turnaround like this fits busy lives and weekday dinners where convenience matters. Sourdough, meanwhile, invites a more leisurely approach. The starter needs maintenance and feeding schedule, and the dough benefits from longer, slower bulk fermentations, often overnight or even longer, which means you plan your bake ahead. This slower fermentation enhances the digestibility of the bread and creates a loaf that can keep fresh longer—but it requires commitment and patience.

Flavor profile pushes this choice even further. Yeast-leavened breads lean clean and simple, providing a blank canvas perfect for sweet doughs like brioche, soft sandwich breads, or those enhanced with herbs, cheese, or spices. The flavor is straightforward, which suits most everyday loaves and recipes that rely on additional ingredients to define taste. Sourdough, on the other hand, offers a robust and tangy zing, often with subtle fruity or nutty undertones depending on the flour and hydration used. The sourdough flavor deepens during long fermentation and baking, and that flavor complexity pairs beautifully with whole grains, rye flour, and denser, hearty bread styles. So if you crave layers of flavor and interest in each bite, sourdough fits that bill perfectly.

Another practical consideration is your kitchen environment and skill level. Commercial yeast doesn't require any special conditions beyond typical room temperature, and it's extremely forgiving. Even if you forget a step or don't perfectly time your proof, yeast breads often still turn out well. Beginners will especially appreciate this reliability. Sourdough starter, however, is a living culture that thrives or struggles based on temperature, humidity, and feeding schedule. Learning to maintain a healthy starter and adjust your process based on how active it is takes time and attention. This learning curve can be part of the joy in baking, but it's something to be aware of before diving in.

Different types of bread also influence whether yeast or sourdough starter fits best. Classic French baguettes, sandwich breads, or basic dinner rolls traditionally rely on commercial yeast for a clean, consistent flavor and an open crumb. On the flip side, those looking to tackle rustic country loaves, pain de campagne, or artisan boules often turn to sourdough because the longer fermentation produces complex taste and a chewy crust with a beautiful crust-to-crumb contrast. Rye breads and mixed-grain loaves also benefit from the acidity of sourdough, which helps break down dense flours and adds shelf life.

Don't forget the health benefits when weighing these options. Sourdough fermentation naturally breaks down phytic acid in the grains, which can improve nutrient absorption and reduce common digestive discomforts. The extended ferment also partially pre-digests gluten proteins, which might make sourdough easier to tolerate for some people sensitive to gluten, though it's not recommended for those with gluten intolerance or celiac disease. Yeast-based breads rise quickly but lack these probiotic and enzymatic benefits. If you're interested in baking bread that aligns with natural food traditions and wellness trends, sourdough offers a wonderful way to connect with these ideas.

From a resource standpoint, commercial yeast is inexpensive, easy to store, and always ready to go. You keep it in the pantry or fridge and grab what you need. Sourdough starter demands a bit more attention—it needs feeding and occasional "refreshing" to stay alive and vigorous. However, once established, a starter can last indefinitely and become a cherished kitchen companion with a unique microbial signature reflective of your home and surroundings. There's something deeply satisfying about cultivating your own starter and baking with it regularly, as it makes bread baking feel personal, almost like an artistic collaboration with nature itself.

In terms of versatility, yeast does have an edge for certain enriched and sweet bread formulas. Because it ferments quickly and doesn't add acidity, it plays nicely with ingredients like sugar, milk, butter, and eggs. Many bakeries and home bakers favor yeast for making brioche, challah, cinnamon rolls, and other tender baked goods. Sourdough can be used for enriched breads too, but the tang can sometimes clash with delicate flavors, or require recipe adjustments. However, if you're willing to experiment, sourdough versions of these breads are possible and richly rewarding once you get the hang of balancing flavors and fermentation times.

Knowing when to reach for yeast or sourdough is part practical, part flavor-driven, and part personal journey. Commercial yeast is the best friend of those who want reliable, speedy results with broad recipe options and beginner-friendly techniques. Sourdough shines when you want to dive deeper, embrace slow food principles, and explore flour, flavor, and texture on a more intimate level. As you build your baking repertoire, don't hesitate to experiment with both. Many bakers enjoy rotating between the two, depending on their mood, time, and desired loaf style.

Finally, remember that neither choice is better or worse—it's about what fits your kitchen, your schedule, and your tastes. Some days you might crave the tangy chew of a sourdough boule; other days, a quick, soft sandwich loaf made with commercial yeast will be the perfect companion to your dinner table. Bread baking is a journey that welcomes all approaches. By understanding the unique qualities and requirements of yeast and sourdough starter, you'll gain the confidence to choose wisely and bake with intent. It's this foundation that will make every loaf you create a joyful and satisfying success.

Understanding Gluten Development is key to mastering the art of bread baking. Gluten is what gives bread its structure, chew, and springy texture—without it, bread would be dense, crumbly, and flat. For those new to baking, grasping gluten's role might seem complicated at first, but it's actually quite approachable once you break it down. It's all about proteins reacting and coming together in the dough, transforming a simple mix of flour and water into an elastic, stretchy network.

At its core, gluten begins with two proteins found in wheat flour: glutenin and gliadin. When water is added to flour, these proteins absorb moisture and start to bond. Glutenin is responsible for dough's strength and elasticity, while gliadin provides extensibility—that ability to stretch without tearing. Together, they create a flexible network that traps the gas produced by yeast during fermentation. This trapped gas causes the dough to rise and develop those lovely air pockets inside the baked bread, giving it a light yet chewy crumb.

What's fascinating is how the process of gluten development isn't just something that happens instantly or passively. It's actively built and improved through mixing, kneading, and sometimes stretching and folding. Each of these actions encourages the proteins to align and link more tightly. Think of it like weaving a fabric: the more you work the dough, the stronger and more cohesive this gluten "fabric" becomes. That's why a well-kneaded dough can be stretched thin without tearing, while under-kneaded dough tends to be slack and fragile.

Still, it's not just about kneading harder or longer. There's a balance you'll want to find—a dough that's developed enough gluten to support structure, but not overworked to the point of toughness. Over-kneading, especially when using a stand mixer, can actually start to break gluten strands down, leading to a crumb that's tight and less tender. For home bakers, a simple test often used is the "windowpane test": gently stretch a small piece of dough between fingers until it's thin enough to see light through without tearing. If it passes, your gluten is well-developed, and you're good to go.

Water also plays a crucial role here. Hydration—the amount of water relative to flour in your dough—affects gluten formation. With low hydration doughs, like typical sandwich bread, the gluten network forms somewhat quickly and is tighter. Higher hydration doughs, common in artisan-style bread like ciabatta or baguettes, have a looser, more extensible gluten network. These wetter doughs are often stickier and harder to handle but reward you with an open crumb and crispy crust. Mastering different hydration levels can take time, but understanding the link between water and gluten strength is the first step.

Salt, which you'll see in nearly every bread recipe, influences gluten development too. Beyond adding flavor, salt tightens gluten strands and slows yeast activity, helping control fermentation and dough strength. It works subtly but effectively to give your dough more resilience, making shaping and handling easier. Just remember: salt should be mixed into the dough after the water and flour are combined to avoid interfering early with gluten formation.

Temperature shouldn't be overlooked either. The warmth of your ingredients and environment affects the rate of gluten formation along with yeast fermentation. Warmer dough strength develops faster, but excessively warm conditions risk overproofing or weakening the dough structure. Cooler temperatures slow things down, giving you more time to develop flavor and texture if you plan for longer fermentation or retardation (refrigeration). Understanding how temperature interacts with gluten development can open doors to more control over your final loaf.

While kneading is the traditional method to develop gluten, there are other gentle techniques that also work, especially for wet doughs. Stretch-and-fold, for instance, delays intensive kneading and lets time combined with gentle folding strengthen gluten. This method is great for home bakers who want to avoid heavy arm work but still achieve well-developed dough. Another approach is autolyse, where you mix just the flour and water and let it rest before adding salt and yeast. This rest period helps initiate gluten bonding naturally without mechanical agitation and often makes the dough more extensible and easier to shape.

It's important to recognize that not all flours behave the same when it comes to gluten development. Bread flour has higher protein content, often 11 to 13 percent, which means it forms stronger gluten networks suited for chewy, structured breads. All-purpose flour generally has less protein, around 9 to 11 percent, so doughs made with it might be softer or less elastic but still fine for many home-baked breads. Whole wheat flour contains more fiber and bran, which can interfere with gluten formation, resulting in denser loaves unless properly balanced with bread flour or special techniques.

As a beginner, it might feel tempting to rush through these steps, wanting immediate results. But taking time to understand and observe gluten development pays off in every loaf you bake. Feel the dough as you knead or fold; note when it shifts from shaggy and sticky to smooth and springy. These tactile cues are invaluable—they guide you more reliably than any timer or recipe step alone. Learning to trust your hands and senses is a rewarding part of bread making that connects you deeply to the process.

One common challenge that new bakers face is dough that is too slack or tears easily. This often points to underdeveloped gluten, which means the dough can't hold its shape or trap gas effectively. The fix usually involves more kneading or additional stretch-and-folds, giving the proteins more time to mesh. Conversely, a dough that's overly tough and resists stretching could mean it's over-kneaded or was mixed too long at high speed. Adjusting your technique until you find that sweet spot of elasticity and extensibility can turn your baking from frustrating to joyful.

Beyond these basics, gluten development affects everything from the crumb structure to the chewiness and even the crust of your bread. A well-developed gluten network supports an open crumb, where you see those beautiful holes and airy pockets inside. It also influences how your bread responds to steam during baking, encouraging a crust that's crisp and well-textured rather than dense and soggy. This science behind the scenes is what transforms humble ingredients into something magical and satisfying.

Remember, gluten isn't a mystery reserved for professionals—anyone can understand it with a little practice and attention. Don't be discouraged if your first loaves don't have quite the texture you hoped for. Each batch is a step forward in tuning your understanding of gluten and how it shapes your bread. With patience, you'll learn to adjust kneading times, hydration levels, and handling techniques to suit your flour, environment, and taste. Soon enough, gluten development will become second nature—a powerful tool in your bread-baking toolkit.

In short, gluten development lies at the heart of bread's structure and character. It's the dynamic, invisible network that gives dough its strength and its chew. Taking the time to learn how to nurture gluten—from choosing the right flour and adding water to kneading just enough and respecting fermentation—makes all the difference in baking bread you'll be proud to share. This foundational understanding sets the stage for everything that comes next in your bread-baking adventures.

Essential Gear for the Home Baker

To get started on your bread-baking journey, having the right tools makes all the difference, but it doesn't have to be overwhelming or expensive. At minimum, you'll want a sturdy mixing bowl, a good-quality kitchen scale to measure ingredients accurately, and a bench scraper to handle dough without sticking. A reliable oven thermometer is essential to ensure your bread bakes at just the right temperature, while a basic baking sheet or Dutch oven can help create the perfect crust and crumb. While high-tech gadgets are tempting, many classic tools do the job beautifully and encourage hands-on learning, which is key to mastering the craft. Investing gradually in these essentials avoids clutter and keeps your workspace inviting—a place where practice transforms from chore to joy every time you bake.

Must-Have Tools (and Budget Alternatives) Getting started with bread baking at home is exciting, but the thought of buying all the gear can quickly become overwhelming—and pricey. Fortunately, you don't need an arsenal of fancy equipment to produce wonderful bread. With a few thoughtfully chosen tools, many of which are quite affordable or cleverly substituted by everyday kitchen items, you can master essential bread-baking techniques without breaking the bank.

Let's begin with the cornerstone of any baker's toolkit: a reliable mixing bowl. You'll want a large, sturdy bowl to combine your flour, water, yeast, and salt—the basic ingredients to every loaf. Stainless steel or glass bowls work wonderfully because they're easy to clean and don't retain odors or stains. These often come in sets, allowing you to have different sizes on hand. However, if purchasing a dedicated mixing bowl feels like too much upfront, a clean, large salad or pasta bowl from your kitchen can double perfectly.

Another essential item is a kitchen scale. Weight-based measurements lead to more consistent, predictable results compared to volume spoons and cups, especially when working with flour and water. This prevents common frustrations like dough that's too wet or dry. While it's tempting to rely on measuring cups and spoons, a digital scale typically costs under $20 and elevates your baking from guesswork to precision. For those entirely against adding a new gadget, measuring cups will do in a pinch— just keep in mind that flour can settle differently depending on how it's scooped.

Flour scooping aside, the next tool worth investing in is a dough scraper. It might seem trivial, but a dough scraper is a game changer when it comes to handling sticky dough or cleaning your workspace. If you don't want to buy a professional scraper, a sturdy plastic or metal spatula or even a flexible putty knife can substitute effectively. Scrapers help you fold dough during bulk fermentation, cut loaf portions, and lift sticky masses off your work surface with ease, all of which reduce frustration and mess.

One of the most iconic and useful bread-baking tools is the banneton or proofing basket. These baskets give your dough structure during its final rise and create those classic spiral or basket-weave patterns on your loaf. While natural rattan or cane bannetons add charm and professionalism, you can also use a clean, well-floured colander, a bowl lined with a clean tea towel, or even a plastic container with slits for airflow. The key is providing the dough with a snug place to rest while keeping it from sticking. Dust your alternative proofing vessel generously with flour to mimic the non-stick characteristics of traditional bannetons.

When it comes to baking, a Dutch oven is hands down one of the best investments for home bakers who want crusty, bakery-style bread. The heavy-duty lid traps steam, encouraging a perfect crust and good oven spring. But don't worry if you don't own one—there are budget-friendly ways to create steam in a regular oven. Simply place a metal pan filled with hot water on the bottom rack or spray the oven walls with water just before loading the dough. If you want something closer to a Dutch oven's effect without the high price, consider a heavy-duty baking stone paired with a roasting pan cover or an inverted metal bowl. These alternatives won't trap steam as efficiently but still help develop crust and improve baking consistency.

Of course, you'll want a reliable baking sheet or pan. Most home bakers use a rimmed baking sheet for loose doughs, rolls, and no-knead breads. These are inexpensive and versatile kitchen workhorses. High-quality non-stick sheets can be slightly pricier but last longer and clean up easier. For budget-conscious bakers, basic aluminum pans or even sturdy cookie sheets from discount stores work fine—just be prepared for potentially less even heat distribution.

Next, consider investing in a bench knife or pastry cutter. This simple tool, with a flat, dull blade and sturdy handle, assists in dividing dough neatly, scraping it from surfaces, and folding it during shaping. Many bakers get by with a butter knife or metal spatula in their kitchen drawer, but if you plan on baking frequently, a bench scraper designed for bread can save time and frustration.

A kitchen thermometer is often underestimated but is invaluable for baking success. Dough temperature affects yeast activity, fermentation speed, and final texture. Measuring water or dough temperature with quick accuracy can eliminate guesswork during mixing and proofing stages. While a professional instant-read thermometer might cost more, inexpensive models designed for cooking meats or candy also work well. If you're tight on budget, paying attention to the feel of your dough and the timing can substitute, but you'll gain confidence and consistency quickly once you start using a thermometer.

Lastly, though it's technically a "nice-to-have" gadget covered in the next sub-section, a dough whisk deserves a mention here. If you prefer a more traditional, hands-off mixing method, a dough whisk helps blend ingredients effortlessly, cutting through sticky dough without overly activating gluten. They are relatively cheap and make mixing dough faster and cleaner. A large wooden spoon or sturdy spatula can stand in as a budget alternative but may require more elbow grease, especially with higher hydration doughs.

Even with all these essential tools, don't feel pressured to buy everything at once. Bread baking rewards patience and experimentation. Starting with just a few core items—even everyday kitchen tools repurposed for bread-making—allows you to explore flavors and textures while saving for specialty gear down the road. You might find that your favorite mixing bowl doubles as your proofing basket or that your trusty baking sheet becomes your bread oven stage.

Spend your money on quality where it truly counts—like a kitchen scale and a sturdy mixing bowl—and balance that with creative budgeting for other tools. Many budget alternatives perform surprisingly well, making bread baking accessible and enjoyable for every kitchen. Remember, the soul of good bread is in the flour, water, yeast, salt, and your hands—not in fancy gadgets. So, build your toolkit gradually, keep your focus on loving the process, and your loaves will thank you.

In short: start with practical, versatile, and budget-friendly tools; choose the essentials that get the job done well; and add specialty gear as your skills advance and your baking repertoire grows. This approach will keep your bread-baking journey joyful, sustainable, and successful.

Nice-to-Have Gadgets for Artisan Results When you're just starting out in bread baking, the essentials provide a solid base: a good mixing bowl, reliable measuring tools, and a sturdy oven. But once those basics are mastered, having a few nice-to-have gadgets can elevate your loaves from simply homemade to truly artisan. These aren't must-haves for every beginner, but they bring precision, efficiency, and a touch of professional polish to your baking adventures. They help to deepen your connection with the craft and add fun elements that can inspire you to try new techniques with confidence.

First on the list, a digital kitchen scale is a game changer. While you might have used measuring cups and spoons, weighing your ingredients leads to much more consistent results. Flour, especially, varies widely in how it packs—scooping and leveling can introduce errors that affect your dough's hydration and texture. A scale takes all the guesswork out and aligns your practice with how professional bakers approach recipes. It's not just about accuracy either; it speeds up prep work and makes scaling recipes up or down easy. If you haven't yet invested, this little tool will quickly prove that it pays for itself in better bread.

Another gadget worth considering is a proofing basket, also known as a banneton. These baskets gently cradle your dough as it rises for its final fermentation, supporting its shape and encouraging a beautiful crust. They come in a variety of shapes—round, oval, and more—that help create loaves that look like they came from a bakery rather than your home kitchen. Plus, the ridges in the basket impress shallow lines on your dough's surface, adding rustic charm when dusted with flour. While you can proof a loaf in a bowl lined with a towel, a banneton develops a superior structure, which is especially important for high-hydration doughs and sourdoughs.

Scoring your bread just before baking is critical to control how it expands and to produce those signature "ear" designs that make artisan loaves so appealing. A simple serrated knife or a lame—a small razor blade holder—can be used, but many home bakers find that a proper bread lame offers precision and ease unmatched by other tools. Its sharp blade glides smoothly over the dough's skin, creating clean cuts that open beautifully during oven spring. Over time, this small gadget becomes an instrument of creativity where your personal marking style becomes a signature, enticing both your eyes and your taste buds before the loaf is even sliced.

For bakers interested in enhancing crust quality and oven spring, a cast iron Dutch oven or cloche deserves a special mention. The heavy lid traps steam released during baking, replicating the humid environment of professional steam-injected ovens. This results in crusts that are crisp and blistered with an appealing crunch while locking moisture inside to keep crumb texture soft and open. Sure, you can bake free-form loaves on a baking sheet, but a covered pot gives you a dramatic leap in artisan quality. Plus, these pots double as perfect tools for roasting vegetables or simmering stews, so they earn their space in your kitchen beyond bread.

Another subtle but valuable addition is a bench scraper. It's a flat, rectangular piece of stainless steel or plastic with a handle, designed to help you handle sticky dough without frustration. While it's primarily a shaping and dividing tool, it also aids in cleaning work surfaces, lifting and folding dough, and even scraping up bits of flour or starter. Many bakers develop an almost tactile rhythm with this tool, as it allows total control over dough manipulation without sticking fingers or tearing strands of gluten. If you have yet to try one, I encourage you to add it to your toolkit—it's surprisingly versatile and a joy to work with once you get the hang of it.

Temperature control is crucial in bread baking, and while using your stove's built-in oven thermometer can suffice, a standalone instant-read thermometer or even an infrared thermometer can really optimize your outcomes. These tools help you monitor not only oven temperature but also your dough's internal temperature at various stages. This insight may sound advanced, but it's invaluable for preventing under- or over-proofing, and achieving a perfect crumb structure. You'll learn how to nudge your fermentation times based on your specific environment, which varies more than most beginners realize. Bringing this sort of precision saves disappointment and surprise during baking.

If you want to explore steam injection beyond the Dutch oven method, a small spray bottle or water pan placed inside your oven works wonders. Controlled steam keeps crusts shiny and crackly by delaying crust formation early in the bake. While these are simple, inexpensive gadgets, they greatly influence your finished loaf. Many artisan bakers swear by steam for that professional bakery crust, and adding a reliable spraying routine is a good stepping stone toward mastering crust textures that sing.

While it might sound indulgent, a dedicated bread blade knife is another nice-to-have, especially for slicing artisan loaves. Their long, serrated edges cut through crust without smashing the delicate crumb inside. Many people underestimate how difficult it can be to perfect a clean slice, especially with boule or rustic hearth breads that have irregular, thick crusts. By investing in this one tool, your presentation and sandwich-making enjoyment improve dramatically. It's such a small detail, but one that fosters pride in your homemade bread, elevating every meal.

Finally, consider gadgets that assist post-baking: a bread box or breathable storage bag keeps your loaves fresh longer by balancing air flow while minimizing dryness. While many bakers store bread in plastic or freezer bags, these tend to soften crusts prematurely. Preserving the crust's crispness and crumb's moisture can prolong the pleasure of your baking efforts across several days, especially in climates with fluctuating humidity. Although these storage solutions don't affect the baking process directly, they complete the artisan experience by ensuring your labor of love tastes its best for as long as possible.

In conclusion, these nice-to-have gadgets aren't about complicating your kitchen or adding expense without reason. They're about enhancing control, confidence, and consistency, which are the pillars of mastering bread baking. They invite you to take small steps to deepen your understanding of how dough behaves and how different tools influence the final loaf. For those who aim beyond the basic loaf—who want to replicate that rich bakery aroma, that crisp crackling crust, and that yield of a perfectly open crumb—these gadgets are companions on that journey. But it's important to remember they're optional. Your hands and your palate are still your most vital tools. These gadgets just provide a little extra encouragement and creative spark.

So when you feel ready to expand your gear, keep these tools in mind. They'll reward your efforts and introduce you to new ways of working with dough, each adding to your growing confidence and joy as a home baker striving toward artisan results.

Core Bread-Baking Techniques

Mastering bread baking starts with understanding a few foundational techniques that transform simple ingredients into something truly delicious. Mixing your ingredients properly ensures everything comes together evenly, and using the autolyse method can give gluten a gentle head start, making the dough easier to handle later. Kneading—or opting for stretch-and-fold or even no-knead methods—develops strength and structure in the dough, which is essential for good rise and crumb. After mixing, the bulk fermentation phase is where flavors deepen and dough doubles in size, while proofing shapes the final character of the loaf. Finally, shaping breads with care and scoring them right before baking controls the oven spring and crust formation, helping you get that bakery-worthy look and texture. These techniques might sound like a lot, but with practice, they'll become second nature and set you up for a lifetime of successful, satisfying bakes.

Mixing & Autolyse Techniques have a huge impact on the quality of your bread and are essential tools in the home baker's repertoire. While mixing might seem simple at first glance—just combining ingredients—it's really the first step in developing the dough's structure and flavor. Autolyse, a French term meaning "self-digestion," is a technique that helps improve gluten development and dough extensibility by hydrating the flour and resting the mixture before adding yeast and salt. Together, these steps set the dough up for success and make the entire bread-making process more enjoyable and rewarding.

When you mix your dough, the main goal is to bring your ingredients together to create a uniform mass with enough gluten development to trap the gas produced during fermentation. If you've ever mixed bread dough straight from the start without much time or thought, you may have noticed how stiff, sticky, or uneven the dough can feel. Good mixing encourages the flour proteins—glutenin and gliadin—to bond and form gluten strands that give bread its characteristic chew and structure.

Traditional mixing methods, like using your hands or a wooden spoon, work great for simple doughs, but even gentle mixing creates friction and heat. Over-mixing at this stage can cause excessive oxidation, which may whiten the dough but strip it of flavor and reduce the natural sugars that caramelize during baking. Mixing isn't just about combining ingredients; it's about nurturing the dough's texture and flavor foundation.

The autolyse technique flips the mixing process by separating it into stages. First, you combine just the flour and water and let this mixture rest for anywhere from 20 minutes to 1 hour. This soaking period allows the flour grains to fully hydrate, swelling and softening them. The enzymes in the flour start breaking down starches into simpler sugars while the proteins begin gently uncoiling, making gluten formation easier. When you add the yeast and salt after the autolyse rest, the dough is more extensible, stretching more easily without tearing. It feels silkier under your hands, and your final loaf will have better oven spring and a more complex flavor profile.

You might wonder, "Is autolyse necessary for every loaf?" For beginner bakers, it may seem like an extra step, but it's one worth mastering early. Especially when working with high-extraction flours like whole wheat or rye, the autolyse helps mellow the coarse texture and reduce dough stickiness. Plus, it can shorten kneading time since the gluten is already partially developed. Not all recipes call for it, but once you give autolyse a try, you'll likely want to make it a regular part of your bread routine.

There's a simple way to get started with autolyse at home. After measuring your flour and water, mix them just enough to incorporate everything evenly—don't worry about kneading yet. Cover the bowl loosely with a towel or plastic wrap and let it rest on your countertop. During this time, you might notice the dough surface looking a bit shaggy or bubbly. That's a good sign; those bubbles mean enzymes have started to work, releasing sugars that will feed your yeast later on.

Once your autolyse is complete, add your salt and yeast—or starter if you're baking sourdough—and mix them thoroughly into the dough. Salt tightens gluten, which slows fermentation but strengthens the dough's overall structure, preventing over-expansion and collapse. Yeast jumps into action after this point, taking advantage of the sugars made available during autolyse. This two-step process balances the dough's texture between elasticity and strength perfectly.

Some home bakers worry autolyse means longer wait times or complicates their workflow, but in reality, it fits easily into most baking schedules. You can mix the flour and water first thing in the morning, let it rest while you go about your day, and return to finish the dough before the first rise. Even shorter autolyse times—around 20 to 30 minutes—

still provide noticeable improvements. Over time, you'll intuitively play with the timing based on the type of bread you want to create and your day's rhythm.

Beyond autolyse, mixing techniques themselves vary widely and can be adapted depending on what tools and time you have. Many bakers use the "fold and stretch" method during mixing to gently develop gluten without heavy kneading. This means you start by combining ingredients roughly, then periodically lifting and folding sections of dough over itself to build tension and trap air. This technique feels less tiring and gives you better control over how much gluten you want to develop, especially for wet or high-hydration doughs.

Mechanical mixers with dough hooks can speed up this step significantly, but it's important not to rely solely on motorized mixing. Overusing the machine can damage gluten strands or cause dough to become too warm, speeding up fermentation more than intended. In contrast, hand mixing gives you subtle feedback about the dough's strength and texture through touch, which is a valuable learning experience when you're starting out.

Once mixing is complete, your dough will feel elastic and slightly tacky to the touch. It should hold its shape like a soft ball but still have enough slackiness to stretch without tearing quickly. Perfecting this feel comes with practice, but autolyse can make the difference by softening the dough's texture and making it more manageable from the very beginning. Many new bakers find their dough less intimidating when autolyse is part of their routine.

In summary, mixing and autolyse are foundational techniques that transform simple ingredients into a living dough capable of incredible flavor and texture. By giving your flour and water time to hydrate before adding yeast and salt, you develop gluten in a gentler, more effective way. Whether you choose to mix your dough by hand, with a mixer, or with stretch-and-fold actions, combining these methods with autolyse elevates even the most basic bread recipes.

As you continue to explore bread baking, pay attention to how the dough changes during and after mixing. The dough's feel, stretch, and responsiveness will guide you toward the best techniques for each loaf. Mixing and autolyse techniques aren't just steps on a checklist—they're moments where you connect with the dough, learn its character, and set the stage for success.

Kneading, Stretch-and-Fold, and No-Knead Methods are fundamental techniques in bread baking that each play a vital role in developing gluten and shaping the texture of your loaf. Understanding these methods will empower you to approach any bread recipe with confidence. Whether you prefer hands-on involvement or a more hands-off approach, mastering these methods helps transform simple ingredients into delicious bread.

Let's start with kneading—the classic method most people picture when they think about making bread. At its core, kneading involves working the dough by hand or with a mixer to develop the gluten network. Gluten is what gives bread its chewy texture and structure. When you knead, you're essentially stretching and aligning proteins in the flour so that they can trap gas produced by yeast fermentation. This process is what lets the dough rise and hold its shape during baking. Although kneading might seem a bit labor-intensive, it offers an immediate tactile connection to your dough, letting you feel when it's ready—smooth, elastic, and slightly tacky but not sticky.

For beginners, kneading by hand might feel unfamiliar at first, but it quickly becomes a rhythmic and rewarding practice. Using the heel of your palm, push the dough away, fold it back over, and turn. Repeat this motion—push, fold, turn—for about 8 to 12 minutes. As you work, the dough will change from shaggy and sticky to soft and smooth. Don't rush it; good kneading takes time and patience. When the dough passes the "windowpane test"—when a small piece can be stretched into a thin translucent sheet without tearing—it's ready for fermentation. This sensory feedback from kneading builds your confidence and connection with the baking process.

However, not every bread dough requires traditional kneading. That's where the stretch-and-fold method comes in, a favorite among artisan bakers. Instead of heavy kneading, this technique encourages gluten development over time during fermentation. It's especially effective for wetter doughs, which can be too loose or sticky to handle easily. With stretch-and-fold, after mixing your dough, you let it rest for a short spell—usually 20 to 30 minutes—then gently lift one edge of the dough and fold it over the rest. You repeat this action several times around the bowl, effectively organizing the gluten strands without risking overworking the dough.

The beauty of stretch-and-fold is that it requires little effort and less time standing at the counter, yet it helps create a strong gluten structure. Typically, bakers incorporate this technique several times during the bulk fermentation period, spaced out over a couple of hours. Each fold improves the dough's strength and gas retention, while maintaining a nebulous, open crumb structure inside the finished loaf. It's a more relaxed approach than kneading, making it perfect if you're baking longer-fermented or hydration-rich breads. Plus, it gently handles the dough, which helps retain moisture and encourages better flavor development.

Now, what if you want to bake bread but have even less time—or just prefer an even simpler method? Enter the no-knead technique, a home baker's game changer. This method relies on a long fermentation period, often overnight or up to 24 hours, to develop gluten without any kneading. When you mix your dough ingredients—flour, water, yeast, and salt—you create a very wet dough that feels almost batter-like. The extended rest allows natural enzymatic activity and yeast fermentation to slowly build that gluten structure and flavor, replacing the need for hands-on development.

No-knead bread has gained immense popularity not only for its ease but for the remarkable artisan-quality crust and crumb it produces. The dough is often baked in a covered Dutch oven or similar heavy pot, which traps steam and promotes a spectacular crust. While the technique demands patience due to long ferment times, the actual "active" work takes just a few minutes upfront. This method is ideal for novice bakers or anyone short on time but wanting to experience homemade bread from scratch.

One common concern with no-knead dough is its slack texture—it can feel too wet to handle at first. But this is normal. Don't be tempted to add more flour; the dough will firm up during fermentation. In fact, the high hydration is a secret to the open crumb—those delightful holes inside the bread—and the crisp, crackling crust. After fermentation, the dough is gently shaped, proofed briefly, then baked. The result is a complex-flavored bread with minimal effort and skill required.

Each of these methods—kneading, stretch-and-fold, and no-knead—comes with unique advantages and fits different baking styles and schedules. If you enjoy getting hands-on and directly engaging with the dough, hand-kneading gives you total control and instant feedback. Alternatively, if you're drawn to artisan techniques but prefer less labor, stretch-and-fold strikes a perfect balance between hands-on and hands-off. And if you're just starting out or need convenience without sacrificing quality, no-knead bread lets you have home-baked goodness with ease and minimal fuss.

You might also notice that these methods affect the bread's texture quite differently. Kneaded doughs tend to create a tighter crumb and chewier texture, perfect for sandwich loaves and breads that need structure. Stretch-and-fold techniques encourage a lighter, airy crust and a more open, uneven crumb that characterizes rustic boules and batards. No-knead loaves usually boast a thin, crisp crust with a moist and open interior, reminiscent of artisan bakery breads. Knowing these distinctions helps you choose the right method for the loaf you want to bake.

One important thing to keep in mind is the role of timing and temperature in all three methods. Kneading develops gluten quickly, so fermentation proceeds swiftly and yeast activity needs to be monitored to avoid over-proofing. Stretch-and-fold spreads gluten development over a longer period, making dough temperature and timing essential for best results. No-knead doughs rely heavily on extended fermentation time at cooler room temperatures or even in the refrigerator, allowing the slow buildup of flavor and structure. These variables might feel tricky at first, but once you get a sense of how your dough behaves in different conditions, you'll develop a natural instinct for it.

Practicing these methods also teaches you to listen to your dough. For example, when kneading, you learn to feel the transition from sticky to smooth. With stretch-and-fold, you watch the dough become more elastic and less rough after each fold. And with no-knead, patience is key—you see a shaggy blob transform into a bubbly, airy mass ready to bake. This attentiveness turns baking into a creative, almost meditative process rather than just following a checklist.

As you gain experience, you might even combine these methods. For instance, some bakers start with a brief kneading to bring ingredients together, then use stretch-and-fold during the bulk fermentation to strengthen the dough without overworking it. Others adapt their no-knead doughs by incorporating gentle stretch-and-folds mid-fermentation to improve texture and handling. Flexibility is encouraged—there are no strict rules in home baking, only techniques you can tailor to fit your taste and schedule.

In conclusion, mastering kneading, stretch-and-fold, and no-knead methods opens up a world of possibilities for your bread baking journey. Each technique has distinct strengths that suit different loaves, time constraints, and skill levels. As you practice, remember these methods are tools to help you develop gluten, create texture, and achieve flavorful results. Embrace the process with curiosity and patience, and your confidence in bread baking will grow with every loaf you pull from the oven.

Bulk Fermentation & Proofing Basics Bulk fermentation and proofing are two cornerstone moments in bread baking, where the dough truly begins to transform into something alive and flavorful. For novice bakers, these stages might feel like waiting rooms with uncertainty, but understanding what's happening during bulk fermentation and proofing will empower you to bake much more confidently. Both processes allow yeast to work its magic, developing the bread's structure, texture, and taste. The subtle art of recognizing when your dough is ready to move on can turn a good loaf into an exceptional one.

Bulk fermentation is the first major rise, right after mixing and kneading, where the dough is left to rest as the yeast ferments and produces carbon dioxide gas. This gas gets trapped within the sticky web of gluten strands, causing the dough to expand and develop strength. At this stage, time and temperature play crucial roles. Warmer environments speed things up dramatically, while cooler spaces slow fermentation and give more flavor complexity due to the extended yeast activity. If you're working in a chilly kitchen, don't worry; just allow a bit more time, and your dough will still come around beautifully.

The duration of bulk fermentation isn't a fixed number etched in stone. Instead, it's about learning to read the dough's signals. It should increase noticeably in size—usually doubling or close to it—and feel airy and somewhat jiggly when gently poked. If it resists or feels dense, it likely needs more time. On the other hand, if the dough collapses or feels too slack, it may be over-fermented. Finding this balance takes practice, but as your intuition grows, you'll develop a feel for the rhythm of the rise that works for your environment and ingredients.

One helpful technique during bulk fermentation is the inclusion of stretch-and-folds. These sets of gentle dough manipulations punctuate the rest period, strengthening gluten by realigning strands and redistributing gas and yeast. Stretch-and-folds don't require the effort of traditional kneading but do more than just resting dough passively. For beginners, incorporating two or three sets spaced 20 to 30 minutes apart makes the dough more resilient and easier to shape later. You'll notice the dough becomes smoother and less sticky as it gains strength.

Once bulk fermentation is complete, the dough is ready for the next stage: shaping and final proofing. Proofing, sometimes called the second rise, is the last crucial pause before baking. During this phase, the dough continues to ferment but at a slightly gentler pace, allowing the loaf to develop final volume and refine its crumb structure. The goal is to puff up gently without exhausting the yeast completely. If under-proofed, the bread won't rise much in the oven— leading to a dense crumb. Over-proofed, and the dough can deflate or become overly fragile, resulting in a flat, overly hollow loaf.

Proofing times vary widely, depending on your recipe, dough hydration, and environment. In warmer kitchens, proofing might only take 30 to 60 minutes, while cooler spaces could require longer. Listening to your dough again is key: when gently pressing your finger into the dough, it should spring back slowly but leave a soft indentation. This "poke test" helps gauge readiness without guessing blindly. For new bakers, don't be discouraged if it takes a few tries to interpret these cues. Bread baking is as much about developing a connection with your dough as it is about following steps.

Temperature and humidity affect both bulk fermentation and proofing significantly. Yeast thrives in warmth, ideally between 75°F and 80°F, but anything over 85°F can speed fermentation too quickly, risking over-proofing. If your kitchen feels cold, try creating a warm proving environment by using a turned-off oven with the light on or placing the dough near a sunny window. Maintaining moderate humidity helps keep the dough surface from drying out during proofing, which prevents an undesirable crust forming too soon. Cover dough with a lightly damp towel or plastic wrap to retain moisture and encourage a soft outer layer.

It's tempting for beginners to rely solely on clocks for timing these stages, but with practice, understanding dough behavior will become your best guide. A well-fermented dough will have a pleasant, slightly yeasty aroma and a soft, almost pillowy texture. You'll start to notice how different recipes and flours change the feel and timing of these rises. High-hydration doughs—those with more water—tend to ferment faster and feel more fragile during proofing, while denser doughs need time for gluten to organize properly.

Another point worth mentioning is the impact of salt on fermentation. Remember, salt is yeast's braking system—it slows down yeast activity, helping to regulate fermentation speed and enhance flavor development. If you skip salt or use too little, fermentation can race ahead, leaving you with dough that's expanded rapidly but lacks depth in taste.

Conversely, too much salt can overly retard yeast, requiring longer proofing and risking underdevelopment. Sticking to your recipe's salt levels is a simple way to keep fermentation on track.

Many home bakers find it reassuring to use a clear container during bulk fermentation. A transparent bowl or container helps observe the dough's rise without disturbing it. You can mark the original dough level with a rubber band or piece of tape at the start so you track progress more easily. This visual feedback offers confidence, especially when rising times vary from recipe guidelines.

After completing bulk fermentation, shaping the dough gently is critical to avoid squeezing out the precious gas that helps give bread its airy crumb. During proofing, being gentle lets the yeast finish their work without exhausting the dough's structure. Remember, the whole point of this waiting game is maximizing flavor and texture, so patience is your essential ingredient here. Baking too soon squashes potential, while giving the dough its due bloom in proofing delivers that satisfying spring and open crumb.

In the world of home baking, there's no single perfect timing for bulk fermentation and proofing. Instead, it's a matter of tuning in to your dough daily, experimenting, and building confidence in what it's telling you. The good news is once you start to recognize its cues—the softness, the aroma, the bounce—the process becomes far less intimidating. You'll quickly see that these two stages, rather than chores, are your dough's moments of transformation where magic quietly unfolds.

As you move forward with recipes, returning to these basics will deepen your understanding and make even complex breads approachable. Bulk fermentation and proofing are where patience pays off in loaf volume, crumb quality, and flavor richness. Every master baker was once here, learning to judge when dough has had its perfect rest. Trust the process—and your instincts—because that's the true recipe for success.

Shaping Loaves Like a Pro is a key part of baking bread that often gets overlooked by beginners but really makes a world of difference in your final loaf's appearance and texture. Shaping isn't just about making your dough look nice—it's about organizing the gluten structure and expelling excess gas so your bread can rise evenly in the oven. When you shape a loaf correctly, you're giving it strength to hold its form during that critical final rise, or proof, which leads to a beautiful crumb and a crust that sings. It might seem intimidating at first, but with some practice and a gentle hand, anyone can learn to shape like a pro.

One of the most important things to keep in mind is that shaping is essentially about tension. Think of your dough as a soft ball of elastic; as you work it, you want to create a smooth, taut surface by stretching and folding the dough underneath. This tension acts like a skin that traps the gases created by fermentation and encourages a well-defined rise. Beginners often handle the dough too roughly or don't build enough tension, which can cause loaves to spread out flat rather than rise tall. So, patience here pays off big time.

Before shaping, your dough will have gone through its bulk fermentation phase where it's enlarged significantly and developed flavor and structure. At this point, it's somewhat delicate but still elastic. Begin by lightly flouring your hands and work surface—not too much flour, or it'll dry out the dough. Gently tip your dough out of its container, pressing it down just enough to deflate large air pockets without squashing the dough completely. The goal is to redistribute the gas evenly to prepare it for shaping.

Start shaping with the most basic and versatile shape— the boule, or round loaf. Place the dough on your work surface and, cupping your hands around the edges, fold the outer parts of the dough toward the center. This folding builds layers and tension underneath the loaf. Once folded, turn the dough seam side down and use the heel of your hand to rotate it while gently pulling it toward you, creating surface tension as the bottom sticks slightly to the counter. This tightening action is key to creating a smooth, taut skin, almost like pulling a drawstring on a bag.

For batards or oval-shaped loaves, the process is similar but involves rolling the dough into an elongated shape. After gently flattening the dough into a rectangle, fold one shorter edge toward the middle, then fold or roll the opposite edge over it to create a cylinder. Pinch the seams tightly to seal, then gently roll the loaf back and forth while rotating it to build tension evenly across the surface. This shaping method ensures your loaf will rise upwards instead of spreading out sideways.

One trick frequently used by professional bakers—and something you should try—is to keep your shaping motions smooth and consistent rather than jerky or rushed. Dough is sensitive; over-handling or rough treatment can knock out too much gas or tear the gluten network, resulting in a dense or uneven crumb. It's easy to get excited or impatient, but slow, deliberate movements will yield the best results. Think of shaping as a dance rather than a chore.

It's also important to adapt your shaping technique based on the type of bread you're making. Higher-hydration doughs, which are more wet and sticky, require a lighter touch and often involve stretch-and-fold methods to create structure before final shaping. Stiffer doughs, like those used in sandwich bread, tolerate firmer shaping to build a tight, uniform surface. As you gain confidence, you'll develop a feel for how different doughs respond under your hands.

Another essential step is sealing your loaf properly. After shaping, the surface should be taut with no visible tears or gaps. Those seams you've folded underneath will be the bottom of your loaf, so tuck and pinch them securely to prevent the dough from opening during proofing and baking. If you notice tiny cracks or holes, patch them with a light pinch or even a dab of water to help the dough stick back together. This final seal keeps everything in place and helps shape the loaf during the oven spring.

While many home bakers shy away from using additional tools in shaping, a bench scraper is often the unsung hero here. This flat, sturdy plastic or metal tool helps you lift, fold, and tighten dough without sticking too much to your hands. It also doubles as a way to scrape loose dough bits off your work surface, keeping things clean and efficient. Investing in a good bench scraper can make your shaping process smoother and quicker.

Once shaped, loaves are usually placed in their final resting spots to proof before baking. This might be a banneton basket, a couche (linen linen cloth), or even a simple parchment-lined baking tray, depending on your recipe and loaf style. Shaping well ensures your dough holds its shape here instead of flattening out or spreading. For round boules, bannetons are wonderful because their ridges help create that classic pattern while supporting the dough's structure. If you don't have one yet, you can mimic the effect by lining a bowl with a floured kitchen towel.

Don't worry if your first few shaped loaves don't look perfect or feel too soft to handle confidently. Shaping takes practice to master, and every dough behaves a little differently. The big takeaway is that gentle but firm tension is your friend—too little and your loaf will spread, too much and you risk tearing. As you bake more, you'll develop an intuitive sense for dough's elasticity and the right amount of pressure to use.

Besides aesthetics and structure, shaping affects the final crumb texture inside your loaf. Proper shaping helps align the gas bubbles produced by fermentation, giving your bread an open, airy crumb that's soft and chewy in all the right places. Poorly shaped dough tends to trap uneven gas, resulting in dense patches or large holes—neither of which are fun when you're biting into your fresh loaf. So while shaping may feel like a small step in the process, it really influences every bite you take.

Lastly, remember to enjoy the tactile experience shaping bread offers. It's a moment to connect with your dough, breathing life into it after hours of waiting. The feel of the dough shifting beneath your fingers, the way it springs back after a gentle poke, even the soft flour dusting your workspace—all these sensory details make bread baking deeply rewarding. With each loaf you shape, you're not just preparing food—you're crafting something nourishing and soulful.

In this section alone, you've learned how to create tension, fold dough effectively, seal your loaf, and consider the unique qualities of your dough. These fundamentals set you up for success across a vast range of bread styles and recipes. With patience and repetition, shaping will become second nature—the bridge between raw ingredients and the stunning, delicious loaf you're proud to share around your table.

Scoring, Steaming & Baking for the Perfect Crust are three essential steps that can transform a simple loaf into a masterpiece, elevating both its look and texture. Once you've mastered mixing, kneading, and shaping, understanding how to properly score, introduce steam, and manage your baking environment ensures the crust becomes irresistibly crisp while locking in moisture for a tender crumb. This section will walk you through these techniques in a clear, approachable way, so your loaves develop that beautiful crust that makes bread baking so satisfying.

Let's start with scoring, often called "docking" or "slashing." Scoring is more than just a decorative touch; it's a practical step that gives control to your loaf as it expands in the oven. Bread dough continues to rise in the intense heat, and without scoring, the crust can burst unpredictably, leaving your bread looking ragged and uneven. Those controlled cuts help direct the oven spring—how the bread expands—resulting in an attractive pattern while preventing cracks in random spots. For novice bakers, mastering scoring might seem intimidating, but with the right tools and a bit of practice, it quickly becomes second nature.

The best tool for scoring is a lame, which is simply a razor blade attached to a handle. Its sharpness and precision allow you to make clean, swift cuts without dragging or tearing the dough. If a lame isn't available, a sharp kitchen knife can work, but ensure it's freshly sharpened and dry to avoid pulling the dough. Typically, cuts are about 1/4 to 1/2 inch deep, depending on the loaf size and dough hydration. The angle of the cut matters too; a slanted cut creates an ear—a raised flap of crust—that's highly desired for artisan loaves. Don't worry about getting perfect artistry on your first loaf; focusing on clean, confident cuts will greatly improve each bake.

Next, steaming your bread during the first part of baking might be the biggest secret to achieving that crisp, glossy crust you often admire at bakeries. Early steam keeps the dough surface moist, delaying crust formation and allowing the dough to fully expand. This results in a thinner, more crackly crust rather than a thick, hard shell. Without steam, the crust can set too soon, restricting oven spring and yielding a dull or overly dense crust. Traditional professional bakeries have steam-injected ovens, but as a home baker, you have some clever workarounds that work just as well.

One easy method is to place a baking tray or pan in the oven as it preheats and then pour a cup of hot water into that pan just after putting your loaf inside. The water vapor creates the necessary steam quickly. You'll want to close the oven door immediately to trap the steam. Some bakers recommend using a spray bottle to mist the oven walls right after loading the bread. Be cautious with this method, as spraying directly onto heating elements can cause damage. Another approach is baking inside a covered Dutch oven or cloche; this naturally traps moisture released by the dough, creating a steaming environment for the first 15 to 20 minutes of baking. Once this initial period passes, remove the lid to allow the crust to brown and crisp up beautifully.

Baking temperature and time directly affect crust development. Most artisan-style breads bake at a high temperature, usually between 450°F and 500°F (230°C to 260°C). This high heat jumpstarts oven spring and caramelization, producing a deep golden crust flavored with nutty, toasty notes. As the crust dries and hardens, sugars and proteins in the dough undergo a reaction called the Maillard reaction, giving that rich color and complex taste. For beginner bakers, preheating your oven thoroughly is critical; a hot oven makes a huge difference in the oven spring and crust texture.

While baking, avoid opening the oven door frequently, especially during the first 20 minutes, since this lets the steam escape prematurely and causes the oven temperature to drop. That sudden chill can interrupt crust formation and affect the loaf's overall quality. Patience is a virtue here—resist the temptation to peek too often; waiting will be rewarded with a gorgeous crust.

Knowing when your bread is done baking relates closely to the crust. You want a loaf with a firm, deeply colored crust that sounds hollow when tapped on the bottom. This hollow sound means the interior is fully baked and not gummy. Using an instant-read thermometer can remove any guesswork; most bread loaf centers reach between 190°F and 210°F when perfectly baked. Overbaking dries out the crumb, while underbaking results in a doughy center and a softer crust.

Crust preferences vary widely. Some people love a thick, crunchy crust that thins out to a paper-like crispness with every bite. Others like a softer crust with just a little chew. Achieving the perfect crust depends not only on technique but also on the flour and hydration level in your recipe. Higher hydration doughs generally produce thinner, crispier crusts due to more steam generated from moisture inside the bread itself. Playing around with hydration and comparing different recipes will reveal your personal crust preference over time.

Cooling your bread correctly is another factor that impacts the crust's final texture. As tempting as it may be to slice into warm bread immediately, allowing the loaf to cool on a wire rack is essential. Cooling lets moisture inside redistribute, preventing the crust from becoming soggy or rubbery. If you wrap bread while it's still warm, steam gets trapped and softens the crust quickly. A well-cooled loaf has a crust that stays delectably crisp for longer, preserving the bakery-quality experience.

Lastly, don't be discouraged if your first few loaves don't have perfect crusts. Even seasoned bakers tweak their steam methods, baking temperatures, and scoring styles to suit different recipes, flours, and ovens. The fascinating part of bread baking is that every loaf teaches you something— whether it's how your oven retains heat or how your hands naturally shape the dough. Keep experimenting with these scoring, steaming, and baking strategies, and soon you'll create crusts that make your bread stand out, both in flavor and appearance.

In summary, scoring gives your bread room to grow and adds visual appeal, steaming produces the much-coveted shiny and crisp crust, while baking temperature and timing lock in color, taste, and texture. Each step is intertwined, and together they bring your bread from just edible to extraordinary. With practice and patience, you'll discover how these simple yet intentional actions turn your kitchen into a bakery that fills your home with irresistible aromas and, best of all, perfect crusts.

Troubleshooting Common Issues

Even the most careful bakers run into problems now and then, so understanding the common pitfalls can help you keep your bread on track. If your loaf collapses or turns out denser than expected, it often points to under- or over-proofing, or sometimes the dough wasn't shaped or handled gently enough before the final rise. Gummy or doughy centers typically mean the bread wasn't baked long enough or the oven temperature was off, while cracked or tough crusts might signal issues with steam or baking time. Keeping an eye on fermentation times and oven conditions, alongside mastering your feel for dough texture, will help you catch and fix these issues early. Storing your bread properly is just as important to maintaining freshness, so once you've nailed your bake, knowing how to freeze or keep it at its best will ensure every slice tastes as good as the first.

Why Did My Bread Collapse? There's nothing more disappointing than pulling a loaf from the oven, only to find it has deflated or collapsed. This sinking sensation can feel like a baking failure, but the good news is that understanding why bread collapses is completely within your reach. Collapsed bread often points to issues in fermentation, gluten structure, or baking technique—but unraveling these causes will help you bounce back and achieve a beautifully risen loaf next time.

The most common culprit behind a collapsed loaf is over-proofing. When bread is left to proof for too long, the yeast ferments all the sugars in the dough, producing more gas than the gluten network can hold. Imagine blowing up a balloon until the rubber gets stretched too thin; eventually, it loses its strength and deflates. In bread dough, over-proofing means the gluten framework weakens as the dough becomes overly airy and fragile, so during baking the structure can't hold the gas bubbles and collapses. The surface may feel soft or even sticky, and the dough may look overly puffy or wrinkled before baking.

Early-stage bakers might get impatient and want to rush the process, thinking proofing faster will save time. But, patience is key; proofing times will vary depending on the recipe, room temperature, humidity, and ingredient activity. Checking your dough with a gentle poke test is a smart habit—if the indentation springs back slowly but partly remains, it's a sign your dough is nicely proofed. If the poke leaves a deep dent that doesn't bounce back, your dough is likely over-proofed and prone to collapsing.

On the flip side, under-proofed dough can cause collapse too, although it usually presents as dense, heavy bread rather than outright sinking. When dough hasn't had enough time to ferment, the yeast hasn't produced sufficient gas to create a stable crumb structure. If you bake too soon, the dough will expand rapidly in the oven with steam and gas produced by yeast, but the gluten won't have enough elasticity to resist stretching, so your loaf can crack and slump down. Think of it as building a house frame without allowing the materials to properly set — it just won't hold up well when stressed.

Another significant factor is gluten development. Gluten is the protein network that traps the carbon dioxide created by yeast, giving bread its structure and chew. If the gluten isn't well developed, your dough won't have the strength to hold the gases, causing a collapse. This can happen if you don't knead or handle the dough enough, or if the flour used has too low protein content for the loaf you're aiming to bake. Your bread will feel weak and slack, and might spread outwards instead of rising upwards.

But bear in mind, gluten development is a balancing act. Too much handling without enough resting can overwork the gluten strands, making the dough too tight and less elastic. This rigidity can hinder gas retention and result in a loaf that bursts unexpectedly in the oven and then collapses. Using the right kneading or folding methods tailored to your recipe helps build a resilient yet elastic dough.

The hydration level—that is, the ratio of water to flour—also influences whether your bread holds its shape during baking. High-hydration doughs, which are wetter and stickier, can produce incredible open crumb and an airy texture. However, if the hydration is too high for the strength of the flour and gluten network, the dough may spread and deflate after baking. Conversely, doughs that are too dry won't expand properly and can lead to dense bread that doesn't rise well. Balancing hydration according to flour type, and gaining hands-on experience with how your dough should feel at different hydration levels, will take much of the guesswork out of the equation.

Temperature during the baking process itself matters as well. If the oven isn't hot enough, or if you place the dough in too early with a cold oven, the loaf won't "set" quickly enough. The initial burst of heat creates oven spring, where the yeast activity spikes and gases expand rapidly, giving bread its lift. If heat is delayed or inconsistent, your bread might rise slowly, weaken, and then collapse. It's worth investing in an oven thermometer to get exact readings, since many home ovens fluctuate or run hotter or cooler than their marked temperature.

Steam during the early minutes of baking plays a subtle but crucial role too. Steam keeps the crust soft, allowing the bread to expand more freely before the crust hardens and locks in the shape. If there's no steam, the crust sets too fast and can limit rise. But too much steam, or too long of a steam phase, might delay crust formation and contribute to weakness in the bread's structure, sometimes making it prone to collapse as it cools.

Ingredient quality can't be overlooked either. Using old or improperly stored yeast, or yeast that isn't active enough, reduces the gas produced, affecting rise and crumb structure. Similarly, salt not only flavors bread but also controls yeast activity and strengthens gluten. Too little salt means looser dough and overactive yeast; too much salt can kill or slow yeast growth—both scenarios risk your bread collapsing.

Some recipes or styles of bread are naturally more challenging and prone to collapse. For example, very high hydration doughs like ciabatta or certain sourdoughs with high water content require gentle handling and proper fermentation to avoid deflation. If you're trying one of these for the first time, don't be discouraged if it collapses; as you familiarize yourself with the dough's feel and proofing signs, your technique will improve.

Finally, keep your expectations flexible. Bread-baking is part science, part art. Environmental factors such as humidity, altitude, and even the flour brand can influence results. Collapse doesn't mean failure—it means an opportunity to learn your dough's needs more intimately. Over time, you'll develop your own intuition about when your dough is ready and how to adjust variables like proof time, hydration, and oven temperature.

Practical steps to prevent collapse start with carefully watching proofing times and obeying the poke test. Use strong bread flour suited for your loaf. Don't rush kneading or avoid it altogether unless using a no-knead method suited for your recipe. Pay attention to hydration and avoid making dough too wet if you don't have experience with slack doughs. Preheat your oven thoroughly, bake on a suitable stone or heavy tray if possible, and create steam in the first few minutes of baking.

Whichever loaf you bake, keep notes about what you changed along the way, from proof times to water amounts to temperatures. Tracking these details is invaluable for troubleshooting and will boost your confidence with each attempt. Collapsing bread is just a signpost on the path toward mastery—it means you're baking, experimenting, and learning. Every baker has been there. Your next perfectly risen loaf is just a proof away.

Fixing Dense, Gummy, or Over-Proofed Loaves It's one of the most frustrating things in bread baking: you pull your loaf from the oven, only to find it dense, gummy, or sadly collapsed from over-proofing. These issues can feel like dead ends, but with patience and a few simple tweaks, you can revive your baking confidence and enjoy beautiful, airy loaves every time. This section will guide you through understanding why your bread might fall into these categories and, more importantly, how to fix and prevent these common problems.

Let's start with dense bread. Dense loaves often result when the dough doesn't develop enough gluten or doesn't have the right balance of ingredients to trap gas properly. Gluten is the protein network that stretches and holds the bubbles of carbon dioxide produced by yeast, creating that light, open crumb you're aiming for. If your dough feels slack or tears easily while shaping, it might lack sufficient gluten development. Often, this happens if the flour you're using has a low protein content, or if the kneading or stretch-and-fold steps were rushed or skipped altogether.

To fix dense bread, focus first on the flour choice. Bread flour with higher protein encourages stronger gluten formation, which naturally leads to a better rise and a more airy crumb. If you only have all-purpose flour on hand, no worries — just be prepared that your bread may be a bit denser by nature. You can still improve it by kneading adequately or incorporating stretch-and-folds during bulk fermentation, which gently builds gluten without exhausting your dough or your arms. If you try these adjustments and your bread still turns out dense, consider lengthening the bulk fermentation. Allowing yeast more time to work means a better rise and more flavor development, but keep an eye so it doesn't over-ferment.

Gummy bread, on the other hand, is a sign that something else is off balance — usually underbaking or excess moisture trapped inside the loaf. You might have baked the bread at too low a temperature, or the internal crumb didn't have a chance to set properly before the crust formed. That's why a loaf can feel wet or sticky when sliced, almost doughy rather than fluffy. A reliable oven thermometer can help ensure your oven is actually at the temperature listed by the recipe, as many home ovens run cooler or hotter than the dial suggests.

One tip to fix gummy bread is to extend the baking time slightly, but don't just throw it back in blindly. If your loaf looks golden but remains gummy, tent it loosely with foil to prevent the crust from burning, then bake a bit longer. Another safeguard is checking the internal temperature of your bread — generally, fully baked loaves reach about 190°F to 210°F depending on the type of bread. Using a simple digital probe thermometer can save you from guesswork. Raising the oven temperature slightly, especially in the last few minutes, can also help the crust caramelize and pull out excess moisture.

Over-proofed bread brings a unique set of problems. It happens when the dough ferments past its ideal point, leading to over-expanded gas bubbles that can't hold their structure during shaping or baking. The result is often a flat, sunken loaf with large air pockets and weak gluten structure. This loaf may even collapse right after going into the oven, and the crumb might feel gummy or wet. Over-proofing often occurs if the dough is left out too long or proofed in too warm an environment, making the yeast overly active and exhausting the natural sugars and gluten network before baking.

Preventing over-proofing always starts with good time and temperature control. Pay close attention to the dough's appearance and feel, rather than simply setting a timer. The dough should look slightly puffed and pass the classic "poke test"—when you press a floured fingertip gently into the dough, the indentation should spring back slowly but not completely disappear. If it springs back immediately, the dough needs more proofing; if it stays indented or deflates, it's over-proofed and should be baked immediately to salvage the loaf.

When faced with an over-proofed loaf, don't despair. One rescue approach is to degas the dough gently by pressing out excess air, then reshaping it and allowing a short, second proof (called a "second proof" or "bench rest"). This usually means only 15 to 30 minutes so the gluten can tighten up and the yeast can generate fresh gas to help your loaf rise again. Keep the environment cooler during this step to slow down fermentation. However, this method works best with firmer doughs; overly slack or wet doughs may not hold shape well after handling and could end up denser.

In some cases, you may decide to bake the dough as-is when over-proofed. While the texture might be more open with some larger holes, the flavor often becomes pleasantly sour or nutty because of the longer fermentation. It's a trade-off, but not a total failure. You can always experiment with slicing techniques or repurposing the loaf—toast or bread pudding can make fantastic secondary uses of denser or gummy bread, turning potential mishaps into opportunities.

Hydration levels play a subtle but vital role in loaf texture, too. High hydration doughs (those with more water relative to flour) tend to produce more open crumbs and tender crusts, but they're trickier to handle and proof properly. Too much water can contribute to gummy crumbs if the loaf isn't baked long enough or if gluten structure isn't strong enough to hold the moisture. Working with high hydration doughs requires confidence in your mixing, shaping, and baking methods—which you'll develop over time. For beginner bakers battling gummy or dense bread, starting with recipes in the 60-65% hydration range is wise before moving up to wetter doughs.

Salt and yeast quantities are other often-overlooked culprits. Salt strengthens gluten and controls yeast activity, so if you skimp or forget it, fermentation can become erratic. Too much yeast speeds up fermentation but risks over-proofing, while too little yeast slows things down and can leave dough under-risen and dense. Accurate measuring and faithful following of recipe amounts will help you find the sweet spot, but don't be afraid to note how your dough reacts in your specific kitchen and adjust from there.

Environmental factors matter a lot, especially for beginners baking at home. Warmer kitchens speed up yeast activity, meaning your dough proofs faster. Conversely, cooler environments slow it down. Knowing this, you can adapt your timing to suit the season or day. If your kitchen feels too warm, try proofing your dough in a cooler spot or for a shorter time. Conversely, if it's cold, give the dough a bit more time under a cover to develop. This flexibility is key to avoiding over-proofed or dense loaves without relying solely on the clock.

One last thought: patience is your best friend in bread baking. Learning to recognize dough readiness by sight and touch builds confidence and reduces the guesswork that leads to many baking pitfalls. Adjusting proofing times, noticing how the dough responds to shaping, and understanding your oven's quirks evolve naturally with practice. Mistakes at this stage aren't failures—they're lessons pushing you toward better bakes next time.

Remember, fixing dense, gummy, or over-proofed bread means treating each loaf like a living thing. Each batch varies with flour, temperature, humidity, and handling. The more you observe and learn from those variables, the more predictable and rewarding your bread baking becomes. With the basics in place and a willingness to experiment, you'll soon unlock the joy of perfectly textured loaves right from your own oven.

Storing & Freezing Bread for Freshness Once you've put in the effort to bake a perfect loaf, keeping it fresh can feel just as important. Without the right storage methods, all your hard work can quickly go stale, dry out, or lose that wonderful crust you worked to achieve. Understanding how to store and freeze bread properly ensures your bread tastes as scrumptious on day three (or day ten) as it did coming out of the oven.

Fresh homemade bread doesn't contain preservatives like store-bought loaves, so it won't last as long on the shelf. That's why a little care is necessary—especially if you're baking larger batches. One common mistake that novice bakers make is wrapping bread tightly in plastic immediately. While it prevents drying out, it also traps moisture, which encourages mold. The key is to find a balance that preserves moisture without suffocating the loaf.

For everyday storage, a paper bag works wonders. It allows the bread to breathe while protecting it from extreme exposure to air that would cause rapid staling. You can also use a bread box, which moderates the environment and helps maintain the right level of humidity. Cloth bags or a clean kitchen towel wrapped around the loaf can serve as a beautiful, natural alternative to plastic and paper, especially for crusty breads like baguettes or boules.

If you find yourself with more bread than you can eat within a few days, freezing is your best friend. Bread freezes exceptionally well because cold halts the staling process and prevents mold growth. But freezing bread properly requires some strategy to lock in freshness and avoid freezer burn. First, be sure your bread is completely cooled before freezing. Wrapping warm bread seals in moisture and leads to a soggy mess when thawed.

When freezing, slice your loaf before wrapping it. This lets you thaw only what you need, reducing waste. Wrap each portion tightly in plastic wrap or aluminum foil. For added protection, place wrapped slices in a heavy-duty freezer bag, squeezing out as much air as possible before sealing. This double-layer approach keeps moisture and freezer odors at bay and helps retain that delicious homemade flavor.

When you're ready to enjoy frozen bread, thaw it slowly at room temperature in its wrapping. For crusty breads, once thawed, a few minutes in a preheated oven or toaster can revive the crust's crunch. Avoid microwaving bread unless you plan to eat it immediately, as it tends to make the crumb rubbery or chewy once cooled.

Some bakers prefer to freeze whole loaves instead of slices. This can work well for denser or sturdier breads—like rye or multigrain loaves—that don't dry out as quickly. Just be mindful that slicing a frozen whole loaf can be tricky, so allow it to thaw for at least a couple of hours before cutting.

It's natural to worry about losing that fresh-baked aroma and texture after freezing, but many home bakers find the small trade-off well worth it to avoid waste. Even flourishes like enriched breads—think brioche or challah—freeze beautifully when wrapped with care. Always remember to label your packages with the date to keep track and aim to use frozen bread within three months for optimal quality.

On the other hand, storing bread in the refrigerator generally isn't a good idea. The cool air actually speeds up starch retrogradation, meaning the bread firms and stales faster than it would at room temperature. While it might seem like a safe middle ground between fresh and frozen, refrigeration usually robs bread of its texture and flavor quickly. Only refrigerate if you live somewhere super humid or if you plan to toast the bread right away.

When tackling common issues related to storage, keep an eye out for humidity and temperature in your kitchen. Warm, damp environments promote mold, while overly dry air causes drying and crumbly bread. If you live where humidity is high, aim to store bread in breathable but protective containers, and consider freezing if you can't eat it right away.

Another small but important tip—resist storing your bread directly on the countertop uncovered. It might seem harmless, but exposure to open air dries out the crumb quickly, turning your soft bread into something closer to cardboard. A simple but sturdy bread box or an airtight container with ventilation holes often makes the biggest difference in prolonging freshness.

Bringing it all together, storing and freezing bread well isn't just about preserving leftovers—it's about savoring your baking successes for longer. Knowing how to give your bread a comfortable "home" after baking means you can bake less often but enjoy fresh bread more consistently. With practice, this step becomes just as rewarding as kneading dough or watching a loaf rise.

Finally, don't be discouraged if your first attempt at storing bread doesn't go perfectly. It's a learning process that even experienced bakers revisit. Try different wrapping materials, freezing methods, or storage locations until you find what works for your home environment. Remember, keeping bread fresh extends not only flavor and texture but also the pleasure of sharing and enjoying your homemade loaves long after you've pulled them from the oven.

Chapter 2
Quick and No-Knead Favorites

—————————— ❯❯❯ ❮❮❮ ——————————

Nothing beats the ease and satisfaction of whipping up bread with minimal effort, especially when you're just starting out and want to see quick results without the fuss of hours of kneading or complicated steps. This chapter dives right into those magic recipes that allow the dough to mostly take care of itself, giving you beautiful crusts and tender crumbs with very little hands-on time. From speedy 15-minute mix-and-bake breads to classic overnight no-knead loaves that develop flavor while you sleep, and one-bowl wonders like batter breads and muffin loaves that streamline the process even more, these favorites are designed to build your confidence and keep your baking journey simple and rewarding. You'll find that these approachable techniques not only save time and effort but also inspire you to experiment with new flavors and ingredients, making baking fun, stress-free, and deliciously accessible.

15-Minute Mix-and-Bake Breads

In the world of bread baking, sometimes you want fresh, warm bread without spending hours or pulling out every kitchen tool you own. That's where 15-minute mix-and-bake breads come in. These recipes are designed for speed, simplicity, and satisfying results, perfect for those moments when you crave homemade bread but don't have the luxury of time or patience. They are an excellent gateway for novice bakers who want to experience the joy of bread baking without the intimidation of complicated steps or long rises.

At their core, 15-minute mix-and-bake breads rely on straightforward techniques and minimal ingredients. You'll often find these recipes using baking powder or baking soda as leavening agents rather than yeast. This switch eliminates the need for lengthy fermentation or proofing, cutting down the bread-making timeline significantly. The trade-off is that the crumb tends to be denser and the texture more cake-like than traditional yeast breads, but the flavor can still be delightfully comforting and fresh out of the oven.

One big advantage here is how approachable these breads are. Because you're not waiting for dough to ferment or rise, mistakes have less time to develop. Over-proofing or under-kneading are non-issues, which removes a lot of the anxiety that can come with yeast bread baking. Mix your ingredients, pour the batter or dough into a pan or onto a sheet, and bake. It's as simple as that. These breads are perfect for quick sandwiches, impromptu guests, or when you just want a warm slice alongside soup or stew in under half an hour.

To get the best from 15-minute mix-and-bake breads, it helps to understand the balance of ingredients. Since these breads are more like quickbreads or soda breads, flour-to-liquid ratios are generally wetter than traditional doughs but firmer than cake batters. It's a delicate balance: too dry and the bread will be crumbly, too wet and it won't hold shape. Experiment a little with different flours—such as all-purpose, whole wheat, or even gluten-free blends—to see how they affect texture and flavor.

One of the most satisfying aspects is how versatile these recipes can be. You can easily jazz up a basic quick bread by adding herbs, cheese, or seeds to the mix, creating savory variations that elevate a simple loaf into a centerpiece. Add fresh garlic and rosemary for a rustic twist, or cheddar and chives for a rich, cheesy bread perfect for brunch. If you're leaning toward sweeter options, a few tablespoons of honey or a handful of dried fruit can transform the bread into a snack or breakfast treat.

Since you'll be stirring most mix-and-bake doughs by hand, it's also a great opportunity to forge a connection with your baking. Feel the texture of the batter as it comes together and listen for the subtle changes in consistency as you add your wet and dry ingredients. Unlike yeast breads, which require patience and waiting for the dough to develop, 15-minute breads invite you to be present, mix, and immediately see—and taste—the results.

It's important to set realistic expectations when starting with these quick breads. They won't have the same open crumb or chewy crust that come with longer fermentation or kneading. Instead, focus on their unique strengths: soft texture, ease of preparation, and reliable success. For many home cooks, this is a brilliant way to build confidence in bread baking and create delicious, wholesome loaves in a fraction of the time.

Timing and temperature are crucial here. Because these breads bake relatively quickly, keep a close eye on the oven to avoid over-baking, which can dry them out. A golden crust signals readiness, while a toothpick inserted in the center should come out mostly clean, though a few crumbs clinging are natural due to the moister crumb. Using an oven thermometer can help maintain consistent temperatures, as quick breads don't respond well to big fluctuations.

Another great benefit of 15-minute mix-and-bake breads is their accessibility. They require very little special equipment—usually just a mixing bowl, spoon or whisk, and a baking pan or sheet. This makes them perfect for those just starting their bread-baking journey or anyone with limited kitchen space. You won't need a stand mixer, proofing box, banneton, or baker's lame to bring these breads to life.

Many of these recipes also adapt superbly to dietary restrictions. Gluten-free flours work well in no-yeast breads because of their inherently different structure and hydration needs. Whether you need to avoid gluten, dairy, or refined sugars, quick mix-and-bake recipes can be tailored with a little creativity. Just keep in mind substitutions might affect texture, so it's helpful to test a batch before making them a regular in your repertoire.

Beyond the ease and speed, quick mix-and-bake breads offer a mental boost. When life gets busy, baking can feel like a chore. These recipes remind us that baking can be quick, joyful, and still deeply satisfying. The smell of fresh bread wafting through your home, however simple the loaf, is a small victory worth celebrating and a perfect confidence builder for taking on more complex breads down the line.

If you're just getting started, try a basic soda bread or quick white bread recipe from this section. See how the ingredients interact, how the dough feels after mixing, and how the bread holds up after baking. Don't hesitate to tweak and add flavors step by step. Once you've mastered the fundamentals here, you'll find it easier to approach longer, slower rising breads with enthusiasm and skill.

It's also worth noting that these breads keep well for a couple of days when stored in an airtight container or wrapped tightly, though like most quick breads, they are best enjoyed fresh. If you want to stretch their lifespan, slice and freeze leftover bread toasting slices as needed. This can make quick breads a handy pantry staple they otherwise might not be.

Ultimately, 15-minute mix-and-bake breads represent a practical, approachable starting point for anyone eager to enjoy homemade bread without a huge time investment. They prove that good bread doesn't have to be complicated or time-consuming, just honest, tasty, and quick to make. Try a few recipes, have fun with the process, and you'll soon see how easily baking bread can become a regular—and rewarding—ritual.

Overnight No-Knead Classics

No-knead breads have become a beloved cornerstone for home bakers who want to enjoy fresh, artisan-style loaves without dedicating hours in the kitchen. Among these, the overnight no-knead classics hold a special place because they combine simplicity with the magic of slow fermentation. If you've ever been intimidated by the thought of kneading dough or nervous about timing, these recipes are for you. They allow the dough to develop flavor and texture gradually while you sleep or go about your day.

The brilliance of overnight no-knead bread lies in its ease and forgiving nature. Simply mix a few basic ingredients—flour, water, yeast, and salt—and let the dough rest covered in your kitchen at room temperature for 12 to 18 hours. This long, slow fermentation enhances flavor and structure, giving you a loaf with a crispy crust and a moist, open crumb that rivals bakery masterpieces. No manual kneading required, just patience and a bit of trust in the process.

What's really encouraging about these breads is that they're incredibly adaptable. Whether you want a classic white loaf or something a little heartier, the basic method remains the same. You can adjust hydration levels for a softer crumb or a chewier texture, tweak fermentation times depending on your schedule, and even experiment with whole grain flours once you feel comfortable. The overnight no-knead technique welcomes beginners and gently guides them to lovely results.

One common concern is often how to shape the dough after its long rest. Unlike traditional bread where shaping happens early, here, the dough will be very loose and sticky—this is entirely normal. Using wet hands or a generous dusting of flour, gently fold the dough onto itself on a floured countertop to form a rough ball. This light handling preserves the bubbles and delicate gluten network formed overnight. Then, you'll place it into a proofing basket or bowl lined with a towel for the final rise before baking.

The baking step itself is surprisingly straightforward but crucial to getting that signature crust and volume. Most overnight no-knead breads thrive in a preheated Dutch oven or heavy lidded pot, which traps steam and creates a hot, humid environment. This mimics professional steam-injected ovens and helps develop a crackly, golden crust. If you don't have a Dutch oven, a heavy casserole or roasting pan can also work with some clever adjustments, like adding a pan of water below the rack to generate steam.

Flavor is often what keeps people coming back to overnight no-knead classics. The extended fermentation time not only develops complexity but also reduces acidity and bitterness sometimes found in faster breads. This results in a mellow, slightly nutty taste with a gentle tang if you let it ferment longer. Your patience, in this case, turns into a deeply satisfying and rich loaf that's perfect for everything from toasted breakfast slices to savory sandwiches.

These loaves are also remarkably versatile once mastered. Because the dough rests ready to bake, you can incorporate seeds, herbs, or olives in the final shaping stage for a flavorful twist. Add a handful of toasted sunflower seeds for a delightful crunch, or mix in rosemary and garlic for a savory savory upgrade. This flexibility means the basic overnight no-knead dough can serve as a jumping-off point to endless variations tailored to your tastes.

For newcomers, the success of overnight no-knead classics can be a real confidence booster. There's no need to worry about over-kneading or under-proofing, and the minimal hands-on time feels so rewarding. You'll quickly learn to trust the slow fermentation and observe how the dough changes over hours, soaking up water and expanding gradually. That relationship with the dough builds a foundation for more ambitious baking adventures.

When it comes to scheduling, overnight no-knead bread fits beautifully into busy lifestyles. Mix your dough before bed, let it rise slowly overnight, and bake the next day with minimal fuss. The warm, fresh smell of baking bread in the morning is a wonderful incentive and a comforting reward. Plus, it eliminates the stress of rushing through multiple steps in one day, giving you fresh bread almost effortlessly.

Of course, practicing these classics will help you develop a more intuitive feel for dough hydration, timing, and temperature, which are key factors in any baking journey.

Pay attention to the texture of the dough at mixing and after fermentation; it should be sticky but manageable and full of air pockets. Don't be afraid if your first loaf is slightly denser or less crusty—these nuances improve with experience, and each bake teaches you something new.

One final tip: the quality of ingredients matters, even for no-knead breads. Using fresh, high-protein bread flour will give you better gluten structure and rise, but all-purpose flour can work well too when you're starting out. Fresh yeast or active dry yeast both perform nicely, but use the one you're most comfortable with. Salt adds flavor and controls fermentation; don't skip it. Also, water quality and temperature affect yeast activity, so lukewarm water is your best friend for mixing.

In summary, overnight no-knead classics offer an inviting way to bake bread that fits within hectic daily routines while still delivering taste and texture that impress. They take the intimidation out of bread baking and replace it with a slow, satisfying rhythm that anyone can follow. Once you master one or two of these recipes, you'll realize the joy of making homemade bread is well within reach—no special skills or fancy tools required.

From the crackling crust to the soft, flavorful interior, these classic breads remind us that sometimes the simplest methods yield the most extraordinary results. So, grab your mixing bowl, combine a few ingredients, and start your own tradition of overnight no-knead bread baking. The rewards—warm, fresh bread and personal baking pride—are absolutely worth it.

One-Bowl Batter Breads and Muffin Loaves

Moving into the realm of one-bowl batter breads and muffin loaves brings a refreshing sense of ease to home baking. These recipes are an excellent starting point for novice bakers who want quick results without the fuss of kneading or multiple steps. The beauty here lies in simplicity. Instead of wrestling with dough, you're working with a wet batter that's mixed all in one bowl, often with nothing more than a spoon or spatula. This approach strips bread baking down to its most approachable form, making it less intimidating and more inviting to anyone new to the craft.

One-bowl batters rely on a high hydration ratio, meaning there's more water or other liquid than you'd find in a traditional dough. This results in a batter that pours or scoops easily into a loaf pan or muffin tins. Unlike classic bread dough that requires developing gluten through kneading, these batters let gluten form naturally as the ingredients rest and bake. This relaxed process yields breads and loaves with tender crumbs and a satisfying crust without any major effort from you. Plus, cleanup is minimal—just one bowl to wash—and that counts for a lot when you're starting out.

What makes these breads really special, beyond the convenience factor, is their versatility. You can keep things simple with a basic white or whole wheat batter loaf, or you can experiment with additions like nuts, seeds, dried fruits, or even chocolate chips to create a personal touch. Muffin loaves are especially handy because they offer that delightful cross between bread and cake. They're perfect snacks, breakfast options, or quick treats to share with family and friends.

Getting the liquid-to-flour ratio right is essential here. Too dry, and the batter won't have the moist crumb we're aiming for; too wet, and your loaf might turn out gummy or flat. Most recipes for these breads fall within a hydration range of about 70 percent or higher, which creates that looser batter texture instead of stiff dough. Often, leavening comes from baking powder or baking soda rather than yeast, which accelerates the process significantly. This leavening gives muffin loaves their characteristic rise and light texture, making them less chewy and more cake-like.

Another advantage of one-bowl batter breads is their forgiving nature. There's less risk of over-kneading or under-proofing because gluten development isn't something you actively manage here. In fact, overmixing the batter should be avoided, as it can lead to tough or dense loaves. Stir your ingredients just until combined, lumps and all. This technique encourages a tender crumb with enough structure to hold together well. The results are satisfying, consistent, and surprisingly impressive for how hands-off the process is.

Let's talk ingredients. Basic batter breads often start with all-purpose flour, though whole wheat or a blend of flours can work beautifully if you want added flavor and nutrition. Sugar or honey—sometimes both—add a touch of sweetness without making the bread dessert-level sweet. Salt enhances flavor and balances the sweetness, while oil or melted butter contributes to moistness and richness. Eggs play a crucial role here as well, acting as binding agents and helping with rise and crumb structure. Dairy like milk or yogurt can also be introduced to tenderize the crumb and add a mild tang.

For beginners, measuring ingredients accurately makes a huge difference. Using measuring cups for liquids and spoons rather than eyeballing helps ensure your batter won't veer off balance. This is particularly important when working with leavening agents. Too much baking soda or powder will give you a bitter taste or an odd aftertaste; too little and your loaf will be dense and flat. Once you get comfortable with the base recipes, you'll develop an intuitive sense for tweaks, substitutions, and variations, but starting precise will give you the best chance at success.

The baking process itself is straightforward. Most batter breads and muffin loaves bake at moderate oven temperatures, typically around 350°F to 375°F (175°C to 190°C). This range allows the batter to set evenly, forming a golden crust as steam escapes and the interior fills out. Muffin pans often require a slightly shorter bake time than loaf pans because of their smaller size. A good way to test doneness is the toothpick method: insert a toothpick in the center and see if it comes out clean or with just a few moist crumbs. If it does, your loaf is ready to come out, no overthinking needed.

Storage is another user-friendly aspect. These batters produce breads that keep well for a couple of days at room temperature when wrapped tightly in plastic or stored in airtight containers. Because these loaves usually contain oil and sometimes eggs, they tend to stay moist longer than usual bread. You can also slice and freeze them, to pull out later as convenient breakfast bites or quick snacks. Thawing gently at room temperature preserves texture nicely, so there is flexibility for meal planning.

One of the biggest motivations for baking these types of breads is the speed with which you can enjoy fresh, homemade loaves. Unlike traditional yeast breads that can require multiple rising periods lasting several hours, batter breads show up on your kitchen counter in under an hour from start to finish. That instant gratification is powerful and encourages you to keep experimenting and baking more often. It's also perfect for busy individuals or families who want wholesome bread without the need to plan days ahead.

It may feel a bit strange at first to toss flour and liquid together without kneading or shaping, but within a few tries, it becomes second nature. This method unlocks the joy of bread baking for those who might have been intimidated by the more technical side of artisan loaves. Plus, batter breads and muffin loaves can be customized in countless ways to suit your taste and occasion—add savory herbs and cheese for a brunch-ready bread or toss in sweet blueberries and cinnamon for a cozy treat with afternoon tea.

Before you dive in, it's worth remembering that the appearance of these breads may not scream 'artisanal bakery masterpiece,' but the flavors and textures often rival more traditional varieties. They bring a homey, comforting quality that's perfect on a quiet morning or shared around the family table. The crumb tends to be tender and moist, with a slightly open structure that's soft but firm enough to slice.

In summary, one-bowl batter breads and muffin loaves are a cornerstone of quick bread baking that set beginners up for confidence and success. They offer an accessible entry point to the joys of homemade bread, with minimal ingredients, fuss-free technique, and wonderful, reliable results. You don't need special equipment—just a bowl, spoon, and loaf pan or muffin tin. The simplicity here is truly liberating.

As you progress through this chapter, keep an open mind to how these breads can fit into your daily routine. Once you understand the basics, you'll find plenty of room to get creative and make these loaves your own. Whether you're seeking fast weekday breakfasts or a charming homemade gift, these batter breads and muffin loaves deliver all the deliciousness with none of the stress.

Chapter 3
Everyday Loaves for Beginners

———————◆◇◆◇◆———————

Baking everyday loaves is where the simple joy of bread-making really begins to shine, offering approachable recipes that don't overwhelm but instead invite confidence and creativity. Here, you'll find straightforward doughs using familiar ingredients—white, country wheat, and easy whole-grain blends—that rise beautifully with minimal fuss, encouraging trial and error without fear of failure. These loaves provide the perfect canvas for learning the rhythm of mixing, fermenting, shaping, and baking, while delivering warm, delicious results that transform your kitchen into a cozy bakery. As you master these basics, including popular varieties like honey oat, potato, and sandwich breads, you build not just skills but a sense of achievement that fuels your passion for baking. Everyday bread doesn't have to be complicated; it thrives on good timing, patience, and the wonderful aroma of fresh bread filling your home, reminding you that baking is a rewarding act anyone can enjoy and perfect with practice.

Simple White and Country Wheat Breads

Moving on from the foundational techniques of bread baking, it's time to explore two of the most comforting and versatile loaves: simple white bread and country wheat bread. These everyday staples are perfect for beginners because they rely on straightforward ingredients and methods, yet yield satisfying results that can become the bedrock of your baking repertoire. Whether you're making sandwiches, toasting up for breakfast, or simply pulling apart a warm loaf to enjoy plain, these breads bring that wonderful homemade touch to your table without any intimidation.

White bread is often thought of as basic or plain, but mastering it is a rite of passage for any home baker. When done well, a basic white loaf is incredibly tender inside, with a golden, slightly crisp crust. The recipe typically calls for all-purpose or bread flour, water, yeast, salt, and sometimes a bit of sugar or fat to enrich the dough. The beauty lies in the simplicity: clean flavors and a soft texture that pairs with just about anything. The process reinforces essential skills—mixing, kneading, fermentation, and shaping—that form a solid foundation before moving on to more complex breads.

On the flip side, country wheat bread introduces a touch more flavor complexity and a subtly heartier texture by incorporating whole wheat flour along with white flour. This combination offers not just richer taste but also a boost in nutrition and fiber, making it a satisfying choice for everyday consumption. Unlike 100% whole wheat bread, which can sometimes feel dense or intimidating for beginners, the blend keeps the loaf light and approachable. Many bakers find this an excellent transition loaf as they grow comfortable with handling whole grains.

Both types of bread follow very similar techniques when it comes to making the dough. You'll start with mixing the yeast into warm water, sometimes with a little sugar to feed the yeast and encourage bubbling activity. Once the yeast is foamy, it's combined with the flour and salt, and occasionally a modest amount of oil or butter is added to enrich the dough. Kneading develops the gluten network that gives bread its elasticity and chew, so take your time here—feel the dough shift under your fingers from sticky and rough to smooth and springy.

Much like a dance, kneading requires rhythm and patience. If your dough is too dry, it won't rise properly; too wet, and it will be hard to shape. One benefit of starting with simple white and country wheat bread is that their doughs are fairly forgiving. You'll get a good sense of how the dough should feel with just a few tries. After kneading, allowing the dough to rest and ferment is where the magic begins as the yeast feeds on sugars and produces gas, causing the dough to rise and develop flavor.

When it's time to shape the dough, remember it doesn't have to look perfect. The goal is a uniform loaf that bakes evenly. For a traditional white sandwich loaf, shaping into a neat rectangle works well. Country wheat bread, on the other hand, lends itself nicely to rounder, rustic shapes, often baked in a banneton or simple bowl before transferring to the oven. While shaping, try to handle the dough gently to keep the air bubbles intact—these bubbles trap the lovely lightness inside your bread.

As you prepare to bake, scoring the top of the loaf with a sharp knife or lame not only creates a pretty appearance but also controls how the bread expands in the oven. For white bread, a couple of simple horizontal cuts suffice. Country wheat loaves may benefit from a cross or an elongated slash along the top. This scoring is more than decorative; it ensures your bread doesn't burst unpredictably and instead enjoys a well-defined rise and crust.

Baking times and temperatures vary slightly between these loaf types, but generally, a medium-high heat (around 375 to 425 degrees Fahrenheit) produces an appealing crust while keeping the interior moist and tender. A steamy oven environment during the first phase of baking helps create a shiny crust with some chew. You can achieve this by placing a pan of water in the oven or spritzing water onto the loaf before closing the door. Simple white bread usually bakes faster because it's lighter, while the denser wheat loaf might need a few extra minutes to cook through.

Once your bread comes out of the oven, resist the urge to slice it immediately. Allow the loaf to cool on a rack; this resting time completes the baking process by letting steam distribute evenly inside, setting the crumb and enhancing texture. Almost every baker learns this the hard way—cut into hot bread, and you'll likely see a gummy, undercooked center. Patience at this stage pays off generously.

One of the most satisfying aspects of starting with simple white and country wheat breads is their adaptability. Feel free to tweak hydration levels slightly or experiment with flour blends once you've nailed the basics. Maybe swap some of the white flour in your country wheat recipe for spelt or rye for a subtle tanginess. Don't be afraid to add a tablespoon or two of honey for sweetness or a knob of butter to the dough for a softer crumb in your white loaf. These breads are a playground for exploring flavor without overwhelming complexity.

When baking these loaves, it's also helpful to keep notes. Track things like rising times, dough feel, or oven temperatures because your kitchen environment—humidity, altitude, temperature—affects the results. Over time, you'll learn how to fine-tune each loaf to your taste and conditions, growing more confident with every bake. This evolving knowledge turns simple baking into a rewarding craft.

For anyone feeling nervous about yeast or kneading, it's worth highlighting how forgiving these recipes can be. Unlike some fancy artisan breads that require strict temperature or timing, simple white and country wheat breads allow room for mistakes and little moments of improvisation. If your dough takes longer to rise, no big deal; just be patient. If you miss a perfectly shaped loaf, that rustic look is charming in its own right. The goal is consistent progress, not perfection.

Finally, let yourself enjoy the process. Bread baking is more than a culinary task—it's a grounding ritual that connects you to the food you eat in a meaningful way. As you develop your skills with these beginner-friendly recipes, you'll build the confidence and intuition needed to venture into more complex loaves in the future. Simple white and country wheat breads will surprise you with their taste and the warmth they bring to your kitchen and home.

In the next section, we will look into other beloved staples like honey oat and potato breads that add richness and softness to your everyday baking list. But for now, mastering these classic, comforting loaves will give you a wonderful foundation to build on.

Honey Oat, Potato, and Sandwich-Style Breads

Now that you've got a handle on the basics of bread baking, it's time to explore some of the truly approachable and delicious loaves perfect for everyday enjoyment— namely honey oat, potato, and sandwich-style breads. These breads have become pantry favorites across many households because they combine softness, subtle sweetness, and versatility in a way that's hard to beat. Whether you're seeking a tender loaf that toasts beautifully or a bread that brings a comforting heartiness to your sandwich, this group of breads deserves a spot in your baking repertoire.

Honey oat bread is a wonderful introduction to baking with whole grains while still keeping things light and fluffy. The oats themselves add a gentle nuttiness and chewy texture both inside the crumb and sprinkled adorably on top, making each slice a little more exciting. What's amazing about oat bread is that it manages to balance nutrition and flavor without any complicated ingredients or advanced techniques. If you've found the texture of whole wheat bread a bit dense or challenging, honey oat might be the perfect stepping stone. Honey, of course, brings in a subtle natural sweetness, which creates a warm aroma as it bakes and keeps the crumb tender and moist far longer than simple white bread.

Potato bread is another excellent choice for beginners looking to elevate their bread-baking skills without intimidation. The secret to potato bread's softness lies in the cooked potatoes incorporated into the dough. These potatoes add moisture and a lovely silkiness to the crumb, resulting in a loaf that stays fresh for days—a blessing if you want to avoid drying out your bread. One of the joys of making potato bread is how forgiving the dough can be through the kneading and rising stages. It's slightly stickier and richer than basic white bread dough, which may feel strange at first, but this quality helps create a cozy, tender loaf suitable for everything from toast to grilled cheese sandwiches.

Sandwich-style breads cover a broad category, but their defining characteristics are straightforward: a fine crumb, soft crust, and a size perfect for layering your favorite fillings. They're designed to be the foundation of countless meals, from simple lunchboxes to hearty weekend brunches. Most sandwich breads feature enriching ingredients like milk, butter, or eggs, which contribute to their soft texture and extend shelf life. The dough is generally easier to handle for beginner bakers because it is more hydrated and forgiving. This hydration, combined with gentle shaping techniques, leads to loaves with an appealing square shape and even crumb, which consistently impress both family and friends.

Getting started with these breads doesn't require specialized equipment or odd ingredients. A basic kitchen scale, a good mixing bowl, and a comfortable oven setup will see you through. Remember, the dough textures of honey oat and potato breads tend to be slightly wetter than standard white bread, so your hands and bench will get a bit stickier. Don't shy away from using a bench scraper or lightly floured hands to help shape the dough without adding too much extra flour. Maintaining the right dough hydration is crucial here; adding too much flour will result in a denser, drier bread that lacks the signature softness these loaves are known for.

One of the reasons honey oat bread is so appealing, especially to those new to bread baking, is that oats themselves are a gentle ingredient. Rolled oats can be swirled right into the dough or sprinkled on top before baking for a rustic look. Some recipes call for soaking the oats in warm milk or water to create a sort of oat slurry; this improves hydration and helps those flakes integrate smoothly into the dough's structure. It's a lovely technique to enhance both crumb and crust, producing a bread that's aromatic and packed with subtle flavor. When you slice into a fresh honey oat loaf, you'll notice a crumb that's tender, slightly springy, and flecked with tiny oat flecks that add texture and visual interest.

Potato bread, on the other hand, offers a little more complexity in how it impacts the dough. Adding cooked, mashed potatoes creates a dough that feels richer and silkier, almost like it has a built-in fat component that mimics the softness butter or milk would bring. Not everyone bakes potato bread, but once you try it, it's hard to forget. You can either fold the potatoes in while the mixture cools or blend them thoroughly with flour to embed them fully in the dough. The moisture from the potatoes will slightly slow the rise, so it's important to be patient during proofing. This gives the yeast ample time to work through the dough and develop both flavor and structure. The subtle sweetness from the potatoes enhances the overall taste, making it a perfect backdrop for savory sandwiches or just a smear of butter.

When baking sandwich-style breads, the shaping stage deserves special attention. These loaves typically rise in rectangular or square pans, and consistent shaping ensures a uniform crumb and even baking. Beginners sometimes rush past this step, but taking your time to gently stretch and fold the dough into shape can make a big difference in the loaf's final size and texture. Once shaped, the dough should feel taut and springy to the touch—neither too loose nor overly tight, which would affect the bread's crumb and rise. Adding milk and a bit of fat, like butter or oil, makes these doughs supple and smooth, enhancing the final crust's tender character and imparting a delicate flavor that's especially appealing to picky eaters and kids.

The beauty of these breads also lies in their adaptability. Don't hesitate to experiment with different oats—steel-cut for a nutty bite, quick oats for a milder profile—or add a sprinkle of seeds like flax, sunflower, or sesame for a slight crunch and nutty aroma. For potato breads, try swapping the standard white potato with sweet potatoes or even purple fingerlings to introduce color and a subtle earthiness. Sandwich breads can be enriched with herbs, cheese, or even small vegetable bits depending on your flavor preferences. Once you've mastered the basic doughs, these customizations will bring a fresh twist and keep your baking adventures exciting.

Many new bakers worry about whether these enriched or grain-infused breads will be too difficult to bake at home, but the truth is they're well within reach for novices. The key is understanding how small changes in recipe components affect dough hydration and rise times. Honey oat and potato breads often benefit from a longer, cooler proofing period to fully develop their flavor without overproofing. Sandwich breads may need slightly warmer, shorter rises thanks to their enriched doughs. Keeping a close eye on dough feel and behavior, rather than just timed clocks, helps build your intuition over time.

It's also worth emphasizing that these breads store beautifully, especially sandwich and potato loaves. Their soft crumb holds moisture and freshness longer than many classic artisan crusty breads, so you can enjoy them over several days without guilt. Just tuck your cooled loaf into a clean kitchen towel or bread box. For longer storage, slicing and freezing is an excellent strategy. Pull out individual slices as needed and toast them directly from frozen for a fresh-baked taste anytime.

As you try baking honey oat, potato, and sandwich-style breads, you'll discover that these loaves fit perfectly into daily life. They don't demand the elaborate timing or temperamental techniques typical of rustic artisan or sourdough loaves, yet they're every bit as rewarding. Each slice filled with your favorite spread or sandwich fixings becomes a comforting reminder that homemade bread is accessible to everyone. There's a satisfying feeling in being able to slice into one of these loaves and see the tender crumb dotted with hearty oats or the silky texture that only a potato-enriched dough can produce.

Above all, these breads encourage patience, care, and a little kitchen creativity. You'll learn to recognize subtle changes in dough feel, smell, and look, building the confidence that turns a simple recipe into a meaningful skill. And once you've nailed your first honey oat or potato loaf, you'll likely find yourself eager to explore beyond, ready to embrace whole grains and other enriched breads with the same enthusiasm. These everyday loaves invite you to enjoy not just the final product but every step of the journey, enriching the kitchen experience and creating moments to savor far beyond just the eating.

So pick a loaf, gather your ingredients, and prepare to bake bread that tastes like comfort and smells like home. The world of honey oat, potato, and sandwich-style breads offers a wonderful place to deepen your skills and fill your table with fresh, heartwarming bread. This is that satisfying territory where beginner bakers become confident ones, and where simple ingredients turn into everyday magic.

Whole-Grain and Multigrain Goodness

Moving beyond the familiar territory of white and simple wheat breads, whole-grain and multigrain loaves open up a world of texture, flavor, and nutrition that transform everyday baking into something truly nourishing. If you've ever found whole-grain breads a bit intimidating or dry in the past, this section is here to set that misconception straight. Baking with whole grains isn't just for health nuts or advanced bakers; it's an achievable, rewarding skill that enhances your homemade bread's character and makes each loaf more satisfying both to the palate and the body.

Whole grains contain all three parts of the kernel: the bran, germ, and endosperm. This makes a profound difference when compared to refined flours, which typically strip away the bran and germ during milling. The bran adds fiber and a nutty flavor, the germ provides protein and vitamins, and the endosperm keeps the carbohydrates. That rich combination is what gives whole-grain breads their distinctive heartiness and complex taste. Plus, the additional fiber can aid digestion and keep you feeling fuller longer—something to appreciate whether you're grabbing a quick sandwich or enjoying bread as a companion to soup or salad.

One of the challenges you might encounter when baking with whole grains is managing the dough's hydration. Because the bran and germ absorb more water than white flour, you'll often need to increase the hydration level in your recipes. This can produce a stickier dough that some may find less manageable at first. But with a little patience and practice, handling these doughs becomes second nature, and the rewards outweigh the initial learning curve. Techniques like autolyse and stretch-and-fold, which you've learned earlier, are especially useful here to develop gluten strength without overworking the dough.

Multigrain loaves go a step further by combining two or more types of grains or flours—such as wheat, rye, barley, oats, or millet—often topped off with seeds like sunflower, flax, or sesame. This blend creates a symphony of textures and flavors in each bite, making every loaf a delightful experience. When mixing your own multigrain dough, take time to consider how different grains and seeds interact. Some grains have stronger flavors or varying water absorption rates, which can affect the dough's consistency and fermentation.

Don't hesitate to experiment with mixing ratios; you don't have to use a ton of whole grains to infuse a bread with character. Even substituting 30 to 50 percent whole grain with white flour can produce an approachable loaf that balances that classic chewy crumb with added depth. If you're aiming for a fully whole-grain loaf, it's best to follow a tried-and-true recipe at first or add a bit of vital wheat gluten to improve structure if your flour's gluten content is lower.

Most whole-grain and multigrain breads benefit greatly from longer fermentation periods, which allow enzymes to break down complex carbs and bring out natural sweetness. If you find the dough tastes a little bitter or the crumb too dense, extending the bulk fermentation or using a preferment like a biga or poolish can help. These steps are gentle ways to coax complexity in flavor while tackling the hearty nature of whole grains.

When it comes to shaping and baking, give whole-grain doughs a little extra care. Because they tend to be denser, scoring isn't just decorative—it helps steam escape and encourages a controlled oven spring. Your baking times might run a bit longer too, so keep an eye on the crust color and test doneness by tapping the loaf's bottom for a hollow sound. Remember, whole-grain crusts tend to brown faster due to their natural sugars, so adjusting oven temperature and baking time to avoid over-browning is helpful.

On a practical level, whole-grain and multigrain breads store well but can dry out or become stale quicker than simple white breads. Storing your loaf in a cloth bag or wrapping it loosely in a kitchen towel maintains a nice balance of moisture and breathability. If you bake frequently, slicing and freezing portions is smart. Toasting slices straight from the freezer will bring back that fresh-baked warmth and crunchy edges, especially with multigrain breads.

One last tip to keep in mind: don't shy away from adding seeds, nuts, or even dried fruit to your whole-grain loaves. These ingredients add distinct bursts of flavor and texture. For instance, toasted sunflower seeds give a satisfying crunch, while adding raisins or chopped dried apricots introduces a gentle sweetness that pairs beautifully with tangy whole wheat. If you're using seeds like flax or chia, soaking them prior to mixing improves their texture and prevents drawing too much moisture from the dough.

Baking whole-grain and multigrain breads is about embracing not just the flavor and nutrition but the opportunity to connect with the tradition of bread-making on a wholesome level. These loaves remind us that bread is more than just sustenance; it's an expression of care and craft. So, approach your next baking session with an open mind, a patient heart, and a willingness to explore. With consistent practice, you'll be amazed at how these naturally rich grains elevate your everyday loaves, turning simple ingredients into something truly special.

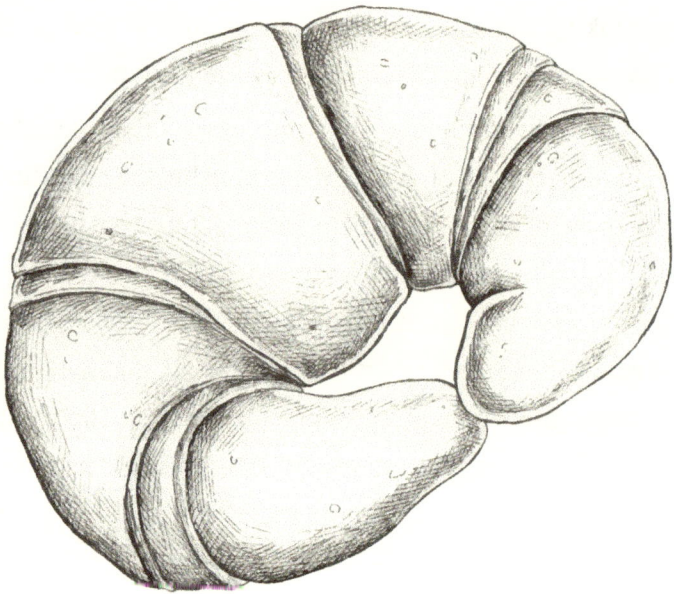

Chapter 4
Sourdough Essentials for Stawwrters

———— »»»⟫ ⟪⟪⟪« ————

Getting your sourdough starter off the ground is truly the heart of creating those tangy, flavorful loaves that many home bakers crave, but starting one can feel intimidating at first. The key is patience and consistency—feeding your starter regularly with the right ratio of flour and water to keep the natural wild yeast happy and active. You'll soon learn to recognize the signs of a healthy starter: bubbly, pleasantly sour, and doubling in size within a few hours of feeding. It's less about precision and more about developing a rhythm that suits your kitchen's environment because temperature and flour type both play their part in the starter's strength and personality. With a good starter on hand, you unlock the door to a world of artisan bread making that's both rewarding and surprisingly accessible, setting the stage for delicious, homemade sourdough loaves that you can be proud of.

Building and Maintaining Your Sourdough Starter

By now, you've likely heard that the heart of any good sourdough bread is its starter—a lively, bubbling mix of wild yeast and friendly bacteria that does the work of fermentation for you. But building a sourdough starter from scratch might feel a bit mysterious at first, like coaxing life out of a jar of flour and water. Fortunately, it's not as complicated as it seems. With patience, consistency, and a little bit of care, anyone can develop a vibrant starter that will provide the unique tang and texture that make sourdough such a joy to bake and eat.

The process begins with just two simple ingredients: flour and water. Choosing the right flour can make a noticeable difference. Whole-grain flours like whole wheat or rye often give your starter a boost because they're rich in nutrients and natural yeasts. These flours tend to ferment faster and develop more complex flavors early on, making them great options for getting your starter off the ground. However, once your starter is established, you can maintain it with plain all-purpose or bread flour if you prefer a milder flavor or a more consistent, predictable rise in your dough.

Here's how the initial phase typically goes. You mix equal weights of flour and water until you have a thick batter-like consistency. The mixture is then left at room temperature, loosely covered, to invite wild yeast and bacteria from the environment to settle in, feed on the flour's sugars, and start multiplying. Within a couple of days, you may notice tiny bubbles forming, a sign that fermentation has begun. This bubbling is your starter's way of telling you it's alive and kicking.

During the first week, feeding your starter regularly is essential to keep these microorganisms happy and growing strong. Feeding means discarding a portion of the starter and adding fresh flour and water to provide new food. While it might seem wasteful to throw some of the starter away, this step is crucial. Without discarding, the mixture would grow unwieldy and too acidic, hindering yeast activity. Feeding every 24 hours allows a balance between fermentation, acidity, and yeast growth to be maintained.

After about 5 to 7 days of consistent feeding, your starter should be bubbly, doubling in size within about 6 to 8 hours after feeding, and have a pleasantly sour aroma like yogurt or mild vinegar. This indicates it's active and ready to help you bake. If your starter shows these signs, you're well on your way to many successful sourdough loaves.

Once your starter is robust, the maintenance rhythm depends on how often you bake. For daily bakers, keeping the starter at room temperature and feeding it every day works well and keeps the microbial community lively. For those who bake less frequently, storing the starter in the refrigerator slows down the fermentation, meaning you only need to feed it once a week or so. Just remember that a cold starter needs to be brought back to room temperature and fed a couple of times before it's strong enough to leaven bread effectively.

One key to maintaining a healthy starter is attention to consistency. Try to maintain a consistent feeding schedule and measure your ingredients by weight for accuracy. While you can recover a sluggish starter with some extra care, erratic feeding habits can lead to unpredictable fermentation and weaker rises in your bread dough. Track the starter's activity after each feeding by noting its rise and fall, and don't hesitate to adjust feeding ratios or frequency if it seems sluggish or overly acidic.

If your starter ever develops an unpleasant smell—like nail polish remover—or shows pink or orange tints, these are signs of contamination. In such cases, it's best to discard the starter and begin anew. Cleanliness in utensils and containers goes a long way in preventing unwanted bacteria or molds from taking hold.

Another useful technique is to adjust the hydration of your starter. Typically, starters are maintained around 100% hydration, meaning equal weights of flour and water. But thicker starters (with less water) or more liquid ones can be experimented with to influence the flavor, fermentation speed, and dough hydration. A thicker starter, for example, may ferment more slowly but develop tangier notes, while a more liquid starter ferments faster and produces a more subtle flavor.

Aside from hydration, temperature plays a powerful role in your starter's behavior. Warmer environments (around 75–80°F) speed up fermentation, resulting in quicker feeding cycles and more pronounced sourness. Cooler temperatures slow activity, which is why refrigeration helps if you're not baking frequently. If your kitchen is chilly, you might find your starter sluggish at first but don't worry—it just needs a little more time and warmth to perk up.

When you're ready to bake, you'll usually "refresh" your starter by feeding it and letting it reach its peak activity just before mixing your dough. Signs of a starter at its peak include a dome-shaped surface, plenty of bubbles, and a pleasant, mildly tangy scent. If you see your starter rising and falling in cycles, the peak is the moment shortly before it starts to fall back down—the ideal time for baking.

Maintaining a sourdough starter isn't just a technical challenge but a rewarding ritual. It fosters a special connection with the bread you bake, as you nurture a living ingredient that, in a way, shares a life cycle with your loaves. Many bakers find this process deeply satisfying because it taps into an ancient tradition dating back thousands of years.

Storage options also offer flexibility. Besides refrigeration, you can dry your starter to preserve it for longer periods. Drying involves spreading a thin layer of active starter on parchment paper, letting it air dry completely, then breaking it into flakes to store in an airtight container. When ready to revive, rehydrate the flakes with water and feed regularly until bubbly again. This method is handy if you need a break from baking but want to keep your starter alive for months.

As you grow more confident with your starter, you might even explore "feeding recipes" that incorporate different flours or hydration levels to influence the flavor and activity. Some bakers enjoy experimenting with rye or spelt to add character, or occasionally increase the starter's hydration to affect crumb openness in their final loaf. This is where the art of sourdough comes alive—beyond the predictable, allowing your personal preferences to shine.

In the end, the key message is that sourdough starters thrive on consistency, attention, and patience. By understanding and responding to your starter's cues—its rise, fall, aroma, and bubble formation—you'll build a healthy culture that supports the kind of bread baking adventures that beginners dream of. And remember, even expert bakers encounter a temperamental starter now and then. Each batch teaches something new about timing, ingredients, and the wonderful microcosm of life you're cultivating right in your kitchen.

Beginner Sourdough Boule Recipes

Now that you've got a solid grasp on cultivating and maintaining your sourdough starter, it's time to put it to work with some beginner-friendly sourdough boule recipes. These recipes are designed to be approachable yet rewarding, guiding you through making round loaves that boast that classic crackly crust and a tender, flavorful crumb. Boules— French for 'balls'—are a fantastic shape to start with. Their round form helps the dough retain moisture during baking, producing a loaf that's both visually stunning and deeply satisfying to slice and share.

Starting with sourdough baking might feel intimidating, but remember: patience and attentiveness are the secret ingredients here. These recipes don't demand perfection right out of the gate. Instead, they build your confidence step by step. With each boule you bake, you'll gain a better feel for the dough's texture, fermentation timing, and how your unique kitchen environment impacts the process.

When you dive into your first sourdough boule, it helps to treat the recipe as a flexible guide rather than a strict blueprint. Flour types, hydration levels, and starter activity can vary, and baking bread is partly an art that invites adaptation. The recipes here suggest reliable starting points, with common baker's percentages and reasonable fermentation times perfect for novice bakers. They'll show you how to handle the dough gently but with purpose—from the initial mix to shaping and baking.

Before mixing your dough, make sure your starter is active and bubbly. This means it's been recently fed and has risen—the signs of yeast and bacteria doing their work well. Using a lively starter guarantees your boule will get a good rise and develop that complex tang we love. If your starter seems sluggish, give it one or two more feedings before baking.

One of the simplest beginner sourdough boule recipes starts with just four ingredients: flour, water, salt, and your starter. This straightforward approach highlights the pure flavor of naturally fermented bread. Using all-purpose flour or bread flour keeps the dough manageable, while the moderate hydration (around 70%) balances softness with structure, making it easier to handle without being sticky.

Mixing the dough is straightforward: combine your flour and water first, allowing an autolyse phase where the flour hydrates—and gluten begins to develop—all before salt and starter enter the mix. This resting step, usually 30 to 60 minutes, makes kneading easier and improves the final bread's texture. Then, gently incorporate your salt and starter, working the dough with stretch-and-fold techniques rather than vigorous kneading. These folds help develop gluten gradually while preserving the dough's delicate bubbles.

Once mixed, your dough will enter bulk fermentation—the time during which the starter ferments sugars, creating gas and flavor. Beginners might worry if the dough doesn't seem to double in size; instead, look for signs like dough that feels puffy, has bubbles on the surface, and springs back slowly when poked gently with a finger. This is a more reliable indication that fermentation is underway. Depending on your kitchen temperature, bulk fermentation often takes between four and six hours, but it can vary.

After fermentation, shaping your dough into a boule is your chance to build surface tension. This step is vital because a taut outer skin encourages good oven spring and a beautifully rounded loaf. You'll practice simple shaping techniques: gently turning and folding the dough until it holds a tight ball shape. Using a floured banneton (proofing basket) or a bowl lined with a kitchen towel helps maintain the loaf's structure during the final rise, called proofing.

Proofing times can be tricky to get right for newcomers. Your dough is ready when it has risen noticeably but still springs back slowly, not too quickly or sluggishly, when poked. To speed things up or slow them down, adjust your proofing environment: a warm spot speeds fermentation; the fridge slows it for overnight proofing, which also helps deepen flavor.

Now, onto baking—arguably the most exciting part. Transferring your boule into a hot Dutch oven or lidded pot traps steam, mimicking a professional steam-injected oven. This steam is essential for a shiny, blistered crust. Preheat your oven and vessel to 450°F (230°C) for at least 30 minutes before baking. Carefully transfer the dough—either by inverting it from the banneton or carefully lifting with parchment paper—then score the top with a sharp blade. Scoring controls how the bread expands during baking and adds a touch of artistry. Bake the boule covered for about 20 minutes, then remove the lid to let the crust crisp for another 20 to 25 minutes.

The result? A boule with a golden, crackly crust and an open-but-structured crumb inside. It's deeply satisfying to twist off a crusty end piece and smell that tangy, yeasty aroma filling your kitchen. Sourdough baking teaches resilience and patience, as every loaf might not be perfect. Some might be denser, some lighter, but every boule brings insight on how your starter, dough, and hands create something nourishing and delicious.

If your first attempts come out dense or flat, don't worry—these are common starter experiences. Try adjusting fermentation times, making sure your starter is vigorous, or being gentler with shaping to preserve air pockets. Remember that every kitchen climate, flour brand, and starter culture is unique. Over time, you'll build intuition and skill, turning these beginner boule recipes into reliable staples for your home baking.

Once you've mastered this foundational recipe, don't hesitate to experiment by incorporating whole wheat or rye flours for added depth, or tweaking hydration for a more open crumb. But for now, focus on mastering the four simple ingredients in harmony with your starter, learning the rhythm of folding, rising, shaping, and baking. Sourdough boule baking is a wonderful journey that blends science and craft, and these beginner recipes lay the groundwork for a lifetime of satisfying loaves straight from your oven.

Whole-Wheat and Rye Sourdough Variations

When it comes to sourdough baking, whole-wheat and rye flours offer some of the most rewarding—and flavorful—variations you can try. They bring depth and complexity to your loaves that white flour alone simply can't match. But they also come with their own set of challenges and quirks that beginner bakers need to understand before diving in. Exploring these grains helps you appreciate the natural diversity of sourdough and how different flours affect fermentation, hydration, and crumb structure.

Whole-wheat flour includes all parts of the wheat kernel: the bran, germ, and endosperm. This makes it richer in fiber, vitamins, and minerals compared to white flour, but also more demanding in bread-making. The bran and germ can interfere with gluten development, making doughs denser and sometimes harder to handle. On the other hand, rye flour behaves quite differently—it contains distinct enzymes and polysaccharides that change the way dough ferments and holds moisture. Rye's gluten is weaker and doesn't develop the same elastic structure as wheat, so it usually results in a more moist, dense bread with a distinct tang and earthy flavor.

One of the first things to keep in mind with whole-wheat sourdoughs is hydration. Whole-wheat flour absorbs significantly more water than white flour, thanks to the bran and germ's fiber content. You'll often find recipes calling for hydration levels of 80% or higher to achieve a dough that's workable and to promote a nicely open crumb. It's tempting to add less water out of fear of a sticky, messy dough, but giving whole-wheat doughs enough hydration will actually make them more manageable and enhance the final loaf's softness and shelf life.

Rye sourdoughs, however, usually require an entirely different approach to hydration. Rye flour doughs tend to be sticky and sticky in a different way from wheat-based doughs. They are often wetter and more fragile, so bakers usually work with a hydration range between 65% and 75%, depending on the rye's coarseness. It's important not to let rye dough dry out because it can quickly turn gummy or tough. Rye's unique sugars and enzymes feed sourdough cultures actively, so fermentation times can be faster and must be monitored closely to avoid overproofing.

The flavor is one of the best reasons to experiment with these varieties. Whole-wheat sourdough brings a nutty, slightly sweet taste that's fuller-bodied than white flour. Rye adds its distinctive earthiness and a hint of spice, which can deepen the sour note typically associated with sourdough. When mixed or used in combination with white flour, both help create more complex, well-rounded flavors in your loaf. Many bakers mix whole-wheat or rye with white flour to strike a balance between taste, texture, and ease of shaping the dough. For example, a loaf made with 20-30% whole-wheat or rye flour mixed with white bread flour offers an approachable way to gain those flavors without sacrificing structure.

Whole-wheat and rye flours also influence how your starter behaves. Rye starters, for instance, tend to ferment quickly and become very active because they contain more sugars readily available to the wild yeasts and bacteria. That means you might feed your rye starter more often or keep it at a slightly cooler temperature to manage its activity. Feeding whole-wheat starters is similar, but they often develop more robust, stable cultures due to bran and germ nutrients. Maintaining these starters well can make baking with whole-wheat or rye flours more predictable, which is especially helpful for new sourdough bakers.

Freshness is another critical factor. Whole-wheat and rye flours have higher oil content (from the germ), which means they go rancid faster than white-flour varieties. Always try to buy these flours in small quantities and keep them tightly sealed in a cool, dark spot—or even refrigerated if you don't bake frequently. Fresh flour will not only improve the flavor of your breads but also help the fermentation process go smoothly.

Working with rye sourdough loaves often leads to experimenting with traditional styles like the Scandinavian and Eastern European rye breads, which usually incorporate a larger proportion of rye flour than typical wheat sourdoughs. Dense and chewy, these breads often rely on longer, slower fermentation and sometimes include added ingredients such as caraway seeds or molasses to complement rye's distinctive taste. They may not puff up like white loaves, but their unique texture and flavor make them incredibly satisfying and nourishing.

When shaping whole-wheat sourdoughs, expect a dough that feels heavier and a little more sticky than you're used to with white flour. It's less elastic but more forgiving in some ways. You might notice your loaf doesn't spring back as much after shaping, resulting in a slightly flatter but still appealing crust. Avoid overworking the dough as the bran in whole wheat can act somewhat like tiny cut grains that break down gluten networks if handled too aggressively. Instead, use gentle stretch-and-fold techniques during bulk fermentation to help develop gluten without roughing up the bran particles.

Time and temperature also play a crucial role for these whole-grain sourdough variations. Bulk fermentation tends to take longer compared to white flour doughs, mainly because the nutrients in whole-wheat and rye flours feed the microbes differently. Rye sourdough might peak much earlier, so eyeing the dough's signs of readiness—including volume changes, feel, and bubble formation—is more reliable than simply timing your processes. Working with a digital thermometer in your dough can be very helpful in managing fermentation temperatures. Cooler room temps slow down activity and are useful if your rye starter or dough is overly aggressive.

There's also room to play with your starter's feeding ratios when working with whole-wheat and rye. A 1:1:1 feed ratio (starter:flour:water) is common for maintenance, but some bakers increase the flour portion to stabilize acidity and encourage a tangier crumb. Especially with rye starters, increasing the feeding amount or frequency can avoid an overly sour or alcoholic flavor that happens when starter sits too long between feedings.

For those eager to boost nutrition while keeping things relatively simple, whole-wheat sourdough is a great choice. It's a perfect blend of taste, health benefits, and approachable technique for anyone moving beyond beginner white breads. Rye sourdough, in contrast, invites you to think differently about your bread-making rhythm and enjoy the rewarding complexity of heritage-style baking. It opens doors to traditional recipes that have fed generations and brings a rustic charm to your home baking that's truly special.

Finally, don't be discouraged if your first whole-wheat or rye sourdough doesn't match your expectations. These flours act differently depending on many factors like batch freshness, starter strength, and even humidity in your kitchen. Baking with them is as much about tuning in to your dough as it is about following a recipe to the letter. Each loaf teaches you something new, and with a little patience, those deeper, flavorful breads will become a beloved part of your baking repertoire.

High-Hydration, Open-Crumb Sourdough

If you've made it this far, you're ready to explore one of the most exciting and rewarding sourdough baking styles: high-hydration, open-crumb sourdough. This style is known for its light, airy interior and irregular holes that make every slice look like a piece of art. It can feel intimidating at first because the dough is wetter and looser than what most beginners are used to, but that's exactly what creates that signature open crumb and delicate texture.

Hydration, simply put, is the ratio of water to flour in your dough. High-hydration doughs typically contain 75% to 85% water—or sometimes even more. This contrasts sharply with lower hydration doughs, which might hover around 60% to 65%. That extra water makes the dough slack and sticky, but it also means the gluten strands can develop more flexibly, forming the network that traps gas during fermentation. The result is a bread that has a wonderfully light and chewy crumb, instead of the tight, dense crumb of a lower hydration loaf.

One thing to remember is that working with high-hydration dough challenges you to rethink how you handle the dough. Traditional kneading to develop gluten simply won't work well here because the dough is too wet to be manipulated in the usual ways. Instead, stretch-and-fold methods become your best friend. These gentle folds strengthen the dough gradually, building structure without tearing the delicate gluten strands. It's a bit like coaxing the dough into shape, rather than forcing it.

Patience pays off when working with this style. You'll often find that high-hydration doughs need longer fermentation times to fully mature. This means you'll need to give your starter ample time to work its magic, creating plenty of bubbles and flavor depth. Bulk fermentation might last many hours at room temperature or slower overnight in the refrigerator, which also helps develop flavor complexity and benefits the dough's structure.

Because the dough is so wet, shaping poses an additional hurdle. Wet dough tends to stick to surfaces and your hands, making it tricky to handle. To tackle this, bakers often use techniques like laminating, where the dough's layers are gently stretched and folded onto themselves during bulk fermentation. Dusting your work surface with flour—or even better, sprinkling some rice flour to prevent sticking—helps tremendously. Using a bench scraper to guide and lift the dough also minimizes direct contact, keeping the dough manageable without deflating all the precious gas bubbles.

Your shaping goal here isn't to create a perfectly tight ball like more traditional sourdoughs. Instead, focus on gently gathering the dough into a loose but somewhat taut round. This ensures it holds its shape without squeezing out too much air. After shaping, use a well-floured banneton or bowl lined with a tea towel to give the dough support as it proofs. This keeps the dough's open structure intact while it rises for the final time.

The baking stage is crucial for high-hydration sourdough because the wet dough can spread out if it doesn't get adequate oven spring. A hot, steamy oven encourages the dough to expand rapidly before the crust sets, locking in that prized open crumb. Starting with a preheated Dutch oven or cloche traps steam and creates the ideal environment for this to happen. You want your oven to be at least 475°F (246°C) when you load in the dough. Many bakers reduce the temperature slightly after the initial burst of steam to avoid burning the crust but maintain oven heat to complete baking.

As the bread bakes, the crust quickly forms a thin, crispy shell that contrasts beautifully with the moist crumb inside. When cooled properly on a wire rack, the crust settles into a perfect balance of crunch and chewiness. Avoid slicing the bread too soon—cutting too early can leave the crumb gummy or sticky. Letting it rest for several hours gives the crumb a chance to fully set, enhancing both texture and flavor.

It's easy to get discouraged with high-hydration sourdough if your first attempts don't produce the dazzling holes you're chasing. But every bake teaches you something about your dough's behavior and the subtle variables at play— from flour brand differences to room temperature, hydration tweaks, and fermentation timing. Even experienced bakers find themselves dialing in these parameters loaf after loaf. The key is to stay curious and keep experimenting patiently.

Your sourdough starter's health also dramatically impacts how well high-hydration dough performs. A vigorous starter with good acidity and activity will aerate wet dough more effectively, creating the gas pockets that result in the open crumb. Feeding routines and starter hydration can be adjusted to encourage a lively environment. Keep an eye on how your starter floats and bubbles during feedings—these are clues to its readiness.

Choosing the right flour is another crucial factor. High-protein bread flour typically handles hydration better and offers more strength, but whole grain flours like whole wheat or rye add flavor complexity and enrich the crumb structure in different ways. You can experiment with flour blends to see what balance of flavor and texture suits your taste and baking style best. Remember, the absorbency and behavior of flours can vary widely, so expect to tweak water amounts as you switch brands or types.

One useful tip is to incorporate an autolyse step for high-hydration doughs, which involves mixing just flour and water and letting the mixture rest for 30 minutes to an hour before adding salt and starter. This rest period helps flour fully hydrate and allows enzymes to start breaking down starches, leading to better gluten development and easier handling of the sticky dough. The dough often feels more flexible and stretchy after autolyse, setting you up for successful folding and shaping.

It's tempting to think a wetter dough might result in a heavier loaf, but in reality, that extra hydration lightens the crumb when handled correctly. Those large, irregular holes are the hallmark of skillfully fermented high-hydration sourdough—and they bring both aesthetic appeal and textural delight to your bread. This crumb mirrors the bread's internal moisture and freshness, making it a joy to tear into at breakfast or assemble into sandwiches.

For novice bakers, mastering high-hydration sourdough may feel like stepping onto a slippery slope at first. But with practice, this style invites you to listen more closely to your dough, noticing its subtle cues and rhythms. You'll develop an instinct for when it's ready to fold, how tautly to shape it, and the exact pop of your oven spring. These lessons build confidence and deepen your relationship with sourdough baking beyond rigid recipes.

Ultimately, the pleasures of high-hydration sourdough come in both the process and the product. Each sticky, wobbly batch carries you closer to a loaf that feels effortlessly rustic yet thoughtfully crafted. The open crumb shows your bread's life inside the oven, revealing the gentle dance of fermentation, gluten, and moisture. It's a delicious reward for anyone willing to step outside the comfort zone of firmer doughs and embrace a wetter, more responsive texture.

Once you're comfortable with the basics, feel free to start experimenting with longer fermentation times or different hydration levels to fine-tune crumb openness and flavor complexity. You might even try incorporating small amounts of add-ins like seeds or nuts—just remember, these can change the dough's hydration needs as well. Watch the dough closely and adjust water gradually until you discover what works best for your kitchen environment and taste preferences.

In time, baking high-hydration, open-crumb sourdough becomes less about precise measurements and more about enjoying the tactile art of bread-making. The dough may be wetter and more unwieldy than what you're used to, but with each fold and rise, it rewards your patience and attentiveness. Before long, you'll find yourself craving this beautiful, springy loaf that combines simplicity with artisanal charm in every bite.

Chapter 5
Artisan and Specialty Loaves

———————— ❯❯❯❯ ❮❮❮❮ ————————

Moving beyond the basics, artisan and specialty loaves invite you to explore breads that are as rewarding to craft as they are to eat, offering a richer variety of flavors, textures, and shapes. These breads often require a bit more attention to fermentation times and hydration levels, but the payoff is well worth it: crusty, flavorful loaves that could easily become the centerpiece of any meal. Whether it's the crisp crust and open crumb of a French baguette or the rustic charm of a German pretzel loaf, these breads teach you new skills while encouraging patience and experimentation. You'll soon find that mastering these loaves adds exciting variety to your baking repertoire, building confidence and expanding your understanding of how different techniques and ingredients shape the final bread. Don't be intimidated— each specialty loaf is approachable once you break down the steps, and the process itself becomes a joyful journey in crafting something truly special at home.

French Baguettes and Pain de Campagne

In the world of artisan bread, few loaves carry the same iconic status as the French baguette and its hearty cousin, the pain de campagne. These loaves represent a beautiful balance of simple ingredients and skilled technique, resulting in breads that are as satisfying to make as they are to eat. Both have deep roots in French baking tradition but offer quite distinct experiences for the home baker. Understanding their differences and how to approach each one can open a new chapter in your bread-baking journey.

The baguette is often what people picture when they think "French bread." Long, slender, and crusty, it's famous for its golden, crackling crust and delicate, airy crumb filled with irregular holes. Despite its seemingly minimalist profile—just flour, water, yeast, and salt—achieving a perfect baguette requires attention to dough hydration, fermentation times, shaping, and baking environment. The baguette's lean dough is high in hydration, which can feel intimidating at first, but don't let that stop you from trying. Once you get the feel for manipulating wet dough and good gluten development, you'll appreciate how the process enhances the baguette's open crumb and crisp texture.

Pain de campagne, often called "country bread," is a more rustic loaf that offers a different kind of satisfaction. It typically blends white bread flour with whole wheat or rye, giving it more depth of flavor and a denser texture. Pain de campagne has a thick, chewy crust and a moist crumb with a slightly tangy flavor, often benefiting from longer fermentation or even a touch of a sourdough starter. This bread is incredibly versatile; it pairs wonderfully with cheeses and charcuterie, but also stands up well to hearty sandwiches. For home bakers, this loaf offers a chance to explore more complex doughs and extended fermentation techniques without the pressure of perfect shaping that comes with baguettes.

One of the reasons these breads remain so popular is how their techniques build on what you've learned from basic bread baking. With a baguette, you'll lean heavily on mastering dough hydration and shaping methods that emphasize tension and structure. The shaping itself—long, slender cylinders—takes a bit of practice but quickly becomes second nature once you know how to stretch and roll the dough properly. Careful scoring before baking allows steam to escape and encourages that beautiful "ear"—the crisp flap of crust that makes slicing the bread so satisfying. Keep in mind that steam created inside your oven during baking is crucial for that glossy, crackling crust, so take the time to create or mimic a steamy environment using a pan with water or a spray bottle.

Pain de campagne offers a slightly more forgiving route. The dough is usually stiffer, which makes shaping into a round boule or oval bâtard easier for beginners, especially since this bread doesn't require the thin, even tension of a baguette. Here you can experiment with autolyse and bulk fermentation, getting a feel for how time and temperature affect gluten development and flavor. If you're using a sourdough starter or prefer a mix of flours, pain de campagne allows you to explore those positively transformative techniques without feeling overwhelmed. The natural flavors that develop over a slow, cool fermentation are a true reward in this bread.

Both breads respond brilliantly to patience. Unlike quick bread methods, these artisan loaves thrive with slower fermentation, which encourages flavor complexity along with better crumb and crust texture. Planning ahead is part of the joy—setting a dough to ferment overnight or longer lets you fit baking into your schedule and see firsthand how dough evolves over time. If your dough feels sticky or tough to handle, remember that increased hydration and slower fermentation often mean you'll be working with wetter doughs. These might stick initially, but light flouring of your hands and workspace, combined with gentle handling, will help immensely.

Incorporating flour variations can be particularly rewarding with pain de campagne. Many traditional recipes use a portion of whole rye or whole wheat, lending a nutty, earthy taste that elevates the rustic character of the loaf. If you're cautious about using rye or whole wheat for the first time, start with a small percentage and observe how it affects fermentation and dough feel. These flours absorb water differently and contribute to gluten structure uniquely, so expect some adjustments—more hydration or longer fermentation might be necessary to achieve a good rise.

Beyond technique and ingredients lies the sensory joy of baking these breads. The sound of a baguette crackling as it cools, the scent of pain de campagne filling your kitchen with warm, wheaty aroma, and the tactile pleasure of tearing into a fresh loaf bring baking from a chore into a ritual. Sharing these breads with family and friends or pairing them with your favorite meals amplifies their value. They encourage mindfulness and patience, two qualities that often carry over to other areas of life, making baking not just productive but restorative.

For beginners, it's tempting to aim for perfect baguettes from the start, but it's more useful to see the process as one of discovery. Don't be discouraged if your first loaf doesn't have the crackly crust or dramatic holes of a bakery baguette. The reality is that many artisan bakers spend years refining these skills. Instead, appreciate how each attempt teaches you more about dough behavior, oven temperature control, and timing. Similarly, pain de campagne, with its heartier profile, invites you to experiment with blends of flour and hydration that will deepen your understanding of fermentation dynamics.

When choosing between the two for your next baking session, think about your current comfort level and what experience you're seeking. Are you drawn to the elegant challenge of thin shaping and high hydration in baguettes, or do you prefer a slower, fuss-free round loaf with complex flavor? Either way, you'll be connecting with centuries-old

French tradition and developing skills that will serve you well beyond this chapter.

Remember, both French baguettes and pain de campagne celebrate simplicity in ingredients but demand respect for time and technique. Baking these breads is not just about filling your kitchen with delicious smells; it's about crafting something timeless. Each loaf carries the story of the baker's patience, care, and attention—a story that can be told again and again with every new bake.

Italian Ciabatta and Focaccia

As we continue exploring artisan breads, Italian ciabatta and focaccia stand out as two iconic loaves that bring rustic charm and incredible flavor to your baking repertoire. Both of these breads boast a rich history in Italy and have found their way into kitchens worldwide, prized for their distinctive textures and versatility.

Ciabatta, which means "slipper" in Italian, earned its name due to its unique shape that resembles a soft, elongated slipper. It's admired for its airy, open crumb structure and thin, crackly crust. One of the reasons ciabatta's crumb is so light and holey is the high hydration in its dough—sometimes upwards of 75% water to flour by weight. This wet dough can feel intimidating at first, but with a few tips and gentle handling, even novice bakers can master it.

Focaccia, on the other hand, is celebrated for its tender interior and slightly chewy texture with a golden, dimpled crust that's often laced with olive oil, sea salt, and fragrant herbs. It's one of those breads that begs to be eaten warm, fresh from the oven, perfect on its own or served alongside soup, salad, or cheese. Unlike ciabatta's elongated shape, focaccia is typically baked in a shallow pan, giving it a thick, robust form that's easy to slice or tear.

Though these loaves differ in shape and crumb, both rely on simple ingredients and well-developed gluten. Flour, water, yeast, and salt remain the core players here, just like with many basic breads. The key to success is understanding how to handle wet, extensible dough to coax out the delicate crumb in ciabatta, or how to create those characteristic bubbles and indentations in focaccia's surface. With patience and practice, you'll get comfortable working with these doughs, gaining confidence as you go.

Starting with ciabatta, it's important to notice that this dough's high hydration means it's quite slack and sticky when mixed. Traditional kneading won't tame it, so bakers often use stretch-and-fold techniques during bulk fermentation. This method strengthens gluten gently without losing the dough's airiness. Perform these folds every 20 to 30 minutes, which also helps redistribute yeast and sugars, promoting better fermentation and flavor development.

Pay particular attention to the fermentation times when making ciabatta. Because of the dough's hydration and yeast activity, under- or over-proofing can dramatically affect your loaf's texture. The dough should roughly double in size, with bubbles visible under the surface, but it should still have some elasticity when gently poked. This balance ensures your bread will rise properly in the oven, forming that desirable open crumb.

Shaping ciabatta loaves is a delicate affair. The dough is too wet to shape tightly like a traditional boule, so handle it carefully using plenty of flour to prevent sticking. The goal is to transfer the dough to a baking surface with as little disturbance as possible to keep those precious gas bubbles intact. Baking on a stone or steel helps create a crisp crust, while preheating your oven with a steaming method can improve oven spring and crust color.

Focaccia, by contrast, embraces a more hands-on shaping process. After mixing and the first fermentation, the dough is spread into a generously oiled pan. This oiling is essential, because focaccia depends on olive oil for its flavor and crust texture. Gently pressing your fingertips into the dough to create dimples is part of the fun—and why focaccia's surface is so distinctive. These little wells capture pools of oil, herbs, and seasoning, creating bursts of flavor and a beautiful rustic look.

Focaccia dough tends to be less hydrated than ciabatta, making it easier to handle, but still soft and somewhat sticky. It typically involves longer fermentation periods that develop layered flavors and a slight chewiness. Using a combination of all-purpose and bread flours can strike a sweet spot between tenderness and strength. The dough's proofing should be slow and steady; it's okay if it's a bit jiggly and padded when pressed—a sign it's ready to bake.

When it comes to toppings, focaccia shines with endless customization. Classic rosemary and coarse sea salt remain top choices for their simplicity and aromatic punch. But don't hesitate to get creative. Sliced olives, cherry tomatoes, caramelized onions, or even thinly sliced potatoes offer delicious variations. Remember to brush the surface generously with olive oil before and after baking to keep the crust wonderfully soft and flavorful—this step elevates your focaccia beyond just bread into a culinary treat.

Both ciabatta and focaccia benefit tremendously from quality ingredients. Opt for unbleached all-purpose or bread flour for better gluten development. Extra-virgin olive oil adds richness and depth to focaccia and even enhances the flavor of ciabatta when brushed on after baking. Fresh herbs and sea salt make a difference you can taste right away. Using filtered water can also help, especially if your tap water has a strong odor or chlorine taste, which might interfere with the yeast.

If you're worried about handling wet dough or longer fermentation times, remember that these challenges are quite normal early on. These breads build skills that will carry over to other artisan loaves and make you a more versatile baker. Stretch-and-fold techniques improve your dough-handling dexterity, and patience during proofing teaches you to read your dough's signals instead of the clock. Each attempt gets you closer to a satisfying, bakery-style loaf at home.

In many ways, Italian ciabatta and focaccia represent the heart of rustic bread baking: simple ingredients transformed by time, technique, and care. They reward gentle hands and the willingness to experiment with hydration, fermentation, and flavor additions. Once you master these loaves, you'll find yourself craving their chewy crumb and golden crusts regularly, eager to share them at meals or as a snack with good company.

Finally, don't be afraid to embrace imperfection. Artisan bread is as much about the journey as the result. Your ciabatta might not be perfectly slipper-shaped on your first try, and your focaccia might have larger-than-expected bubbles or slightly uneven dimples. That's part of what makes each loaf unique and yours. With every bake, you'll be growing your skills and deepening your connection to the craft of bread making.

Enjoy the process and the delicious rewards that come with making Italian ciabatta and focaccia part of your kitchen routine. These breads offer a wonderful opportunity to dive into Italian baking traditions and bring a little taste of Italy into your home.

German Pretzel Loaves and Rolls

Among the many beloved breads of Europe, German pretzels stand out for their distinctive deep brown crust, chewy interior, and the unmistakable sprinkle of coarse salt. Pretzel loaves and rolls bring this iconic treat from the snack table to the dinner table, offering a hearty, rustic bread option that's both visually striking and delicious. If you're new to baking and intrigued by artisan breads with character, mastering pretzel loaves and rolls is a rewarding challenge that will expand your hands-on skills while introducing you to some traditional baking techniques unique to Germany.

The key to authentic pretzel bread lies primarily in how it's prepared before baking. Unlike many breads that go straight from proofing to the oven, pretzels undergo an alkaline bath—usually a quick dip in a baking soda or lye solution. This step might sound intimidating at first, but it's essential since it triggers the Maillard reaction that gives pretzels their trademark deep dark crust and slightly glossy sheen. For home baking, a boiling soda bath is a safe and straightforward alternative to the more traditional lye, which requires precise handling.

Once the loaves or rolls are dipped in the alkaline solution, they are sprinkled with coarse salt that partners beautifully with the slightly tangy, firm crust and soft crumb inside. The salt isn't just a garnish; it plays a key role in balancing flavors and adding texture to every bite. Pretzel breads are traditionally made with simple ingredients—flour, water, yeast, salt—but their preparation technique elevates them far beyond an everyday white loaf.

To get started with a basic pretzel dough, you'll notice that the hydration tends to be lower than some other rustic breads. This gives the dough a firmer, more elastic feel, which is easier to shape into the characteristic pretzel twists or rounded rolls. Since the dough isn't overly wet, it's actually quite beginner-friendly—it's less sticky and easier to handle, especially when you're learning how to shape and proof shaped doughs properly.

When shaping rolls or larger loaves, maintaining a smooth surface is important to achieve an even coloring during baking. For pretzel rolls, rolling into tight balls and letting them rest before the soda bath helps develop a tender but structured crumb inside. For loaves, an elongated or braided shape works well, helping the dough bake evenly and improving the visual appeal on your table. Pretzel twists are an excellent introduction if you want to recreate the traditional shape, but don't be afraid to get creative with little rolls or even pretzel sticks once you grasp the basic dough.

Proofing is another step where patience pays off. Pretzel dough benefits from a final rise that is just enough to become puffy but not overly proofed, as that could result in a pale crust and less chewy interior. The warm environment encourages the yeast to work steadily without rushing, which brings out subtle flavors along with that perfect crumb texture. You'll find that this stage shapes the difference between a rustic pretzel roll and a flat, dense piece of bread.

When it comes to baking, oven temperature and timing take on added importance. High heat is crucial to the signature crust development, typically around 425°F to 450°F (218°C to 232°C). Your oven ideally should be preheated thoroughly to give that initial burst of steam and heat, which results in the crisp outer shell that crackles when you break into the bread. Plus, using a baking stone or an inverted baking sheet can help distribute heat more evenly and mimic a professional deck oven effect right in your kitchen.

One of the joys of pretzel breads is how versatile they are at the table. Pretzel rolls make fantastic sandwich carriers, especially for heartier fillings like roast beef, mustard, or melted cheese. The dense crumb holds up well without becoming soggy, unlike softer sandwich breads. Pretzel loaves sliced thick create a rustic accompaniment to stews, sausages, or rich spreads, enhancing every meal with their bold flavor.

Before taking on pretzel baking, it's helpful to become familiar with your dough's feel and elasticity, as this gives you great control during shaping. Since pretzel dough is not kneaded as aggressively as some other breads, you can expect a chewier, denser texture—perfect for that authentic bite. Don't be discouraged if your first batch looks less glossy or brown than the pretzels you buy at the bakery; like most breads, this takes practice and a feel for your particular oven and environment.

Cleaning up after the baking soda bath is simple but important. You don't want any residue left on your baking tools or trays, as baking soda can build up over time. A quick rinse and wipe down prevent build-up and keep your pans shiny for the next batch. This little extra care ensures your pretzel breads continue to bake beautifully without sticking or burning.

One way to make pretzel baking even more exciting is to explore variations. Some bakers add a touch of malt syrup or sugar to the dough for a bit more sweetness beneath the savory crust. You can also experiment with toppings besides coarse salt, such as sesame seeds, poppy seeds, or even freshly cracked black pepper. These options give your pretzel breads a personal twist while still respecting tradition.

In summary, German pretzel loaves and rolls offer an inviting challenge for home bakers looking to step beyond everyday bread recipes. The process emphasizes attention to timing, shaping, and that unique alkaline bath, which together create a bread that's as delicious as it is eye-catching. With patience and a few simple ingredients, you'll soon be pulling golden, crusty pretzels right out of your oven, ready to impress family and friends with your artisan baking talents.

Next time you sit down for a meal or plan a gathering, consider reaching for homemade pretzel rolls or an impressive loaf. With each bake, your skills will grow, and your confidence will too, proving that even the most iconic specialty breads are well within the reach of a motivated home baker.

Seeded, Sprouted, and Heritage-Grain Breads

In this section, we move into a flavorful and nutrient-rich world where the choice of grain plays a starring role in the character and health benefits of your bread. Seeded, sprouted, and heritage-grain breads aren't just a treat for your taste buds—they offer an opportunity to connect more deeply with traditional baking and wholesome ingredients that elevate your loaf beyond the everyday. Whether you're curious about adding texture and crunch with seeds, enhancing digestibility through sprouted grains, or exploring the robust flavors of heirloom varieties, this chapter will help you get comfortable with these special kinds of bread.

Seeded breads, for starters, are a fantastic way to introduce complexity and nutrition to your baking without needing any complicated techniques. Seeds like sunflower, pumpkin, flax, sesame, and poppy are common favorites. They add a delightful crunch and a nutty aroma, but they also bring valuable nutrients such as healthy fats, fiber, and proteins. When including seeds in your recipes, it's important to know that some are better toasted for flavor while others shine best raw. Toasting seeds before mixing them in your dough enhances their aroma and crunch, making the bread irresistibly aromatic, but it's optional depending on your preference.

Add seeds inside the dough or sprinkle them generously on top before baking for a rustic, artisanal look. One simple approach is mixing a handful of mixed seeds right into your dough during the final stretch-and-fold phase or after kneading. They hold their texture beautifully and lend an extra bit of interest with every bite. For a visually impressive crust, brushing the loaf lightly with water before pressing seeds on top helps them stick during baking.

Moving on to sprouted grains—these offer an exciting twist in bread baking. In essence, sprouting grains involves soaking and allowing the kernels to begin germination before grinding them into flour. This process unlocks enzymes that break down some of the starches and gluten, leading to a bread that feels lighter and easier to digest. Sprouted-grain breads have a slightly sweet, nutty flavor and a moist crumb, which many find more enjoyable than traditional whole-grain breads. Also, because some starch is converted during sprouting, the bread often has a slightly lower glycemic index, making it a bit friendlier for blood sugar regulation.

Sprouted grains can be purchased in flour form or as whole sprouted kernels. Adding these into your baking routine might take a bit of experimentation since they absorb moisture differently compared to regular whole wheat or white flour. You may find the dough more hydrated, and it might require slightly less kneading or different handling during fermentation. But the rewards—a tender crumb packed with wholesome nutrients—are well worth the extra step.

If you'd like to try sprouting your own grains at home, it's quite straightforward. The process starts with rinsing whole grains like wheat berries, rye, or spelt, then soaking them in water for several hours, and finally draining and rinsing twice daily until tiny sprouts appear—usually within two to three days. Once sprouted, you can dry them gently and grind them into fresh flour or fold the damp sprouts directly into your dough, bearing in mind that this method affects hydration and fermentation.

Heritage-grain breads offer a fascinating journey into the past, showcasing ancient varieties of wheat and other cereals that modern agriculture has largely replaced with hybrids bred for higher yields. These grains—including Einkorn, Emmer, Khorasan (often known by the brand name

Kamut), and ancient rye—carry a unique flavor profile and nutritional benefits. Their kernels tend to be smaller, denser, and richer in protein and micronutrients compared to typical bread flours. Breads made from heritage grains often boast a fuller, earthier taste with mild sweetness, making each bite interesting and complex.

Baking with heritage grains may challenge you initially because their gluten behaves differently from modern wheat. The gluten in Einkorn, for example, is more delicate, requiring gentler mixing and a more careful fermentation process. This means doughs can be stickier and less elastic, but with patience and attentive technique, you'll produce loaves with a wonderfully tender crumb and heightened flavor depth. Don't be discouraged if your first attempts feel tricky—these grains aren't the easiest to master but are well worth the effort.

When working with heritage grains, consider blending them with strong bread flours to balance flavor and structure. For example, combining Einkorn or Emmer with a portion of high-protein bread flour helps support gluten development and produces a loaf that's easier to handle. Alternatively, blending sprouted heritage grain flour with modern whole wheat flour can add nutritional complexity while keeping dough management straightforward.

Seeded, sprouted, and heritage-grain breads each contribute something special. Seeds bring texture and bursts of flavor; sprouted grains offer gentler digestion and subtle sweetness; heritage grains connect us with the history and tradition of bread, introducing rich, complex flavors. Together, they invite you to experiment, adjusting hydration, fermentation times, and mixing methods to find the perfect balance.

For beginners, it's helpful to start with recipes that incorporate one element at a time. Try baking a simple seeded loaf first, mixing in a variety of seeds into a basic whole wheat or white dough. Feel how the seeds distribute and how they change the crumb. Next, branch into sprouted grain bread using store-bought sprouted flour or sprouted kernels. Watch for changes in dough texture and flavor, making small hydration adjustments as needed. Lastly, take on a heritage grain recipe, perhaps blending ancient grains with your usual bread flour for a manageable transition.

Don't be afraid to expect some trial and error here. These breads respond to their ingredients' unique characteristics, seasonal variations, and your specific kitchen environment. You'll learn how to interpret dough feel and rise times, noticing the subtle differences that seeds, sprouts, and heritage grains introduce. Ultimately, this kind of bread baking rewards your care and curiosity with loaves that are not only stunningly tasty but nutritionally satisfying and rich with tradition.

Embracing these breads also opens a door to a more sustainable and mindful approach to ingredients. Many seed varieties are easy to source locally or organic, sprouted grains reduce anti-nutrients like phytic acid, and heritage grains promote biodiversity by supporting rare, ancient plant varieties. Baking seeded, sprouted, and heritage-grain breads is a way to nourish your body, delight your senses, and honor the agricultural roots of bread itself.

Now that you've discovered the unique qualities each brings to the table, it's time to grab your mixing bowl and experiment. These breads might take a bit of extra time and attention, but the result—a wholesome, flavorful loaf brimming with character—is sure to inspire your continued baking journey.

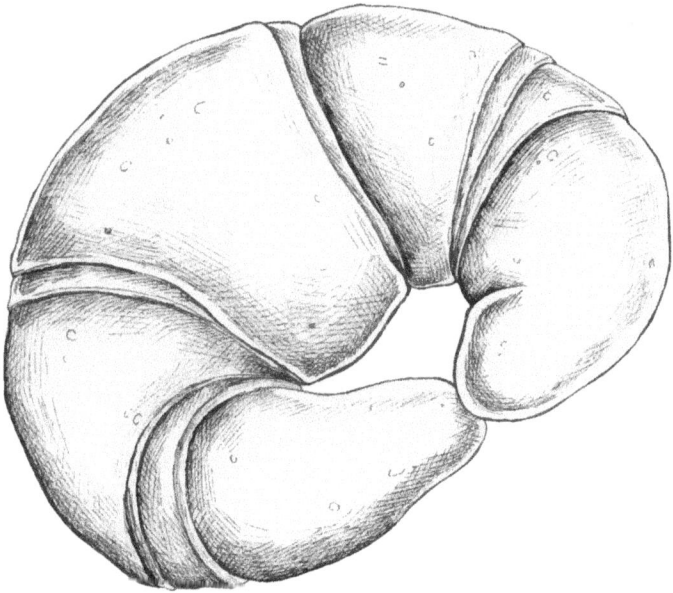

Chapter 6
Enriched, Sweet, and Festive Breads

B read baking takes a delightful turn when you venture into enriched and sweet varieties, where ingredients like butter, eggs, milk, and sugar come together to create soft, tender textures and richer flavors that feel like a treat every time you bite in. These breads often carry a festive spirit, perfect for celebrations or cozy moments, and while they might seem intimidating at first, their rewarding results are well worth the effort. You'll find that mastering these recipes involves gentle kneading and patient proofing to achieve that signature fluffiness, while incorporating spices, fruits, or chocolate adds layers of warmth and indulgence. Whether it's the shiny golden crust of challah or the swirls of cinnamon in a babka, these breads invite creativity and joy, encouraging you to take your basic skills from ordinary loaves to irresistible, crowd-pleasing classics that bring sweetness both to your kitchen and your gatherings.

Brioche, Challah, and Milk Bread

When diving into enriched breads, few loaves capture the imagination and delight quite like brioche, challah, and milk bread. These breads are a step up from your everyday loaf, featuring ingredients that elevate their texture, flavor, and overall richness. They're perfect for special occasions or simply as a treat to enjoy with breakfast or afternoon tea.

The defining characteristic of these breads is the use of enriched dough—that means flour is combined not only with yeast, water, and salt but also with eggs, butter, sugar, and sometimes milk. Together, these ingredients create dough that's soft, tender, and flavorful, with a crumb that almost melts in your mouth. Unlike many rustic breads, the crumb here is fine and delicate, and the crust tends to be golden and glossy, often thanks to an egg wash.

Juggling enriched dough can feel intimidating at first, especially because the fats and sugars can slow down yeast activity and make the dough feel heavier. But with a bit of patience, and a few simple tricks I'll share, baking these loaves becomes absolutely doable—even for beginners.

Let's start with brioche. This French classic is the epitome of richness. Imagine a buttery, slightly sweet bread with a tender crumb that's perfect for everything from decadent French toast to a fancy sandwich. The traditional dough calls for plenty of butter and eggs, which results in a dough that's soft and sticky. That sticky, buttery dough might seem tricky, but it's actually quite manageable once you understand its behavior during kneading and proofing.

One key to working with brioche is patience during kneading. Because of all the fat, the dough won't develop gluten as quickly as a lean dough will. You'll notice it feels soft and a bit slack, but don't be tempted to add more flour to stiffen it up. Instead, trust the process and keep working the dough; it will gradually come together into a smooth ball. You can also use a stand mixer if you have one—it makes this step much easier and less messy. The dough should finally become shiny, elastic, and still a bit soft to the touch.

Once your brioche dough is ready, it needs a good bulk fermentation and then a second rise in the pans or molds. This slow, steady fermentation allows the dough to develop flavor and structure. Also, handling enriched dough with gentle hands is crucial to keep the air bubbles intact, which makes for a light crumb.

Challah, on the other hand, brings a different kind of richness and a cultural story. This traditional Jewish bread is not only delicious but also beautifully braided. Learning how to braid challah dough is a rewarding experience, producing a loaf that's as lovely as it is tasty. The dough is enriched with eggs and a little oil, which keeps it soft but gives it a slightly different flavor profile compared to brioche's buttery richness.

Challah dough tends to be a bit less sticky than brioche, which means it's often easier for beginners to work with. It still requires enough kneading time to develop elasticity but doesn't have the same heavy butter content to slow the process. Because challah often has a glossy crust, brushing it with an egg wash before baking is essential—this adds color and a slight sheen that makes the loaf look almost jewel-like.

When shaping challah, the braid is central not just for its aesthetic appeal but also because the strands bake together to form a loaf that pulls apart in tender sections. Mastering the three-strand braid is a great place to start, and from there, you can experiment with more complex braids as you gain confidence. Watching the dough puff up beautifully in the oven is one of the most satisfying moments in bread baking.

Milk bread, often associated with Asian baking traditions, takes a slightly different approach. The dough is often enriched with milk, giving it a subtle sweetness and a velvet-soft texture. This bread feels incredibly tender thanks to the milk proteins and sometimes a bit of fat from butter or oil.

You might come across recipes calling for tangzhong—a cooked flour and water paste—that's stirred into the milk bread dough. Tangzhong helps retain moisture, so the final loaf stays soft and fresh longer than usual. This technique is fascinating because it's a little bit like science meets tradition, providing impressive results without extra fuss.

Milk bread is famously used for sandwich loaves or soft dinner rolls. Its fine crumb and slightly sweet flavor make it perfect for a variety of uses, from simple sandwiches to serving with butter and jam. The dough is forgiving and relatively easy to handle, making it a favorite first enriched bread for bakers who might find brioche or challah too intimidating at first.

Despite these differences, brioche, challah, and milk bread share certain similarities worth highlighting. All require a bit more attention than lean breads—they demand gentle kneading, careful proofing, and often benefit from an enriched environment to rise properly, like a warm, draft-free spot. The enriched ingredients also mean these doughs store differently and benefit from being consumed relatively fresh or frozen if not eaten right away.

Another tip is to resist overbaking. Because these breads include sugar and fats, they brown faster than simpler bread doughs. Watching closely towards the end of the baking time ensures you won't dry out the crumb or get a crust that's too thick. Many bakers like to tent the bread with foil halfway through baking if it's browning too quickly but still needs time to finish cooking inside.

Baking these breads at home does more than fill your kitchen with irresistible aromas; it connects you to a deep tradition of comfort and celebration. Brioche, challah, and milk bread might seem fancy, but their recipes reward your effort with loaves that feel like small triumphs. You'll find that baking them builds your skills, from working with enriched dough to mastering shaping techniques.

As you gain experience, you can start experimenting—adding raisins or nuts to challah, or turning brioche dough into buns for burgers or sliders. Milk bread can be shaped into pull-apart loaf forms or sweet rolls, each variation opening new doors to exploring texture and flavor.

This trio of enriched breads also fosters creativity in the kitchen, offering flexibility whether you're aiming for an elegant dinner centerpiece or an everyday snack that feels a bit special. The essential lesson is that with just a few extra ingredients and a small shift in technique, your bread baking jumps to a whole new level—both in taste and in the joy it brings.

Remember, the path to mastering enriched breads like brioche, challah, and milk bread is gradual. Begin with the basics, don't rush proofs, and learn to trust your dough. It will tell you what it needs. Treat these breads with care, and you'll be rewarded with loaves that look stunning and taste even better—breads that invite smiles, sharing, and moments worth savoring.

Cinnamon Swirl, Babka, and Chocolate Loaves

Once you've mastered the basics of enriched doughs and the simpler sweet breads, you're ready to dive into some truly delightful and impressive treats: cinnamon swirl, babka, and chocolate loaves. These breads combine enriched dough's tender crumb with rich fillings and beautiful shapes that make every loaf feel like a celebration. They're not just tasty—they're showstoppers perfect for weekends, holidays, or whenever a cozy, sweet pull-apart bread is in order.

At first glance, these breads might seem intimidating, especially if you're new to incorporating fillings and creating swirled or twisted shapes. But breaking down the process reveals it's really about layering simple dough skills with flavorful additions and taking your time with the shaping steps. Think of it like art: the dough is your canvas, and the filling is your paint. By combining them carefully, you'll create stunning breads that look and taste like you spent hours perfecting them, even if you haven't.

Cinnamon swirl breads are a wonderful introduction to this technique. The dough is soft and buttery, still slightly elastic from the proper gluten development you've worked on in earlier chapters. The defining feature is the rich cinnamon-sugar filling, which you spread thinly over your rolled-out dough before rolling it into a log. When baked, the sugars caramelize and cinnamon infuses the crumb, resulting in a tender bread with pockets of warm spice and just the right amount of sweetness. The key to success here is evenly distributing the filling without overloading so the dough maintains its structure during baking.

Rolling the dough tightly but gently is essential. You don't want to squeeze out the filling, but you also want a nice compact swirl that will bake through evenly. After rolling, slicing the log into individual rolls or making a loaf with a spiral reveals those beautiful cinnamon ribbons inside. These breads reward precision in each step, whether measuring ingredients or monitoring proof times, but don't be discouraged if your first attempt isn't perfect. Like any new skill, the magic comes with practice.

Babka takes cinnamon swirl's concepts and turns them up several notches, adding intricate twists and a more decadent flavor profile. Originating from Eastern European Jewish baking traditions, babka is a rich, yeast-leavened loaf filled with chocolate, cinnamon, or other sweet pastes that gets braided or twisted before baking. Its dramatic look comes from cutting the rolled dough down the middle lengthwise and twisting the two halves together so the filling peeks through in delicate ribbons. This creates a stunning visual mosaic that also influences texture. Some bites are dough-heavy and tender while others are pockets of fudgy, intense filling.

Chocolate babka is a particular favorite for many bakers. Using a luscious chocolate filling made with cocoa powder, sugar, butter, and sometimes chocolate chips elevates the loaf into indulgence territory. One common tip is to keep the filling cool but still pliable so it spreads easily but doesn't soak right through the dough. Otherwise, your loaf might become soggy or lose its shape. Using good-quality chocolate or cocoa powder can turn a simple home bake into something with bakery-level flavor.

Don't rush the shaping stage for babka. The twisting technique can feel fiddly at first, but it's what sets the loaf apart. View it like braiding hair: start slow, hold the dough gently, and trust that your hands will get the hang of it. After shaping, the final rise is crucial to ensure your loaf puffs up beautifully and the filling softens into those irresistible swirls. When baked, the babka's crust caramelizes around the filling, giving you contrasts of crispiness and gooey richness.

Chocolate loaves, while sometimes overlapping with babka, can also refer to simpler versions incorporating chocolate chips or chunks scattered throughout a tender enriched bread dough without the intricate shaping. These loaves are perfect if you're looking for something less technical but still want that sweet, chocolatey reward. Because the dough is enriched with butter and eggs, the crumb is soft and moist, providing a delightful backdrop to the richness of melted chocolate inside.

One important balancing act for chocolate loaves is ensuring the deck-level sweetness doesn't overwhelm the bread. If the dough is too dense or packed with too much sugar, it can become gummy after baking. So sticking to measured amounts for both dough enrichment and chocolate additions is essential. Using a dough that's slightly firmer than for cinnamon swirl breads can also help support the weight and distribution of chocolate pieces.

For all three of these enriched, sweet, and festive breads, patience tops the list of ingredients. Because enriched doughs contain sugar and fats, proofing times can be longer or a bit more sensitive to temperature than lean doughs you might have tried earlier. It's normal for the dough to feel more relaxed and sticky—this means you've added enough butter and eggs to develop that tender crumb. Using a warm, draft-free spot will help your dough rise steadily without overproofing.

As you approach baking these breads, keep an eye on crust color. Because of their sugar content, enriched breads brown faster, so you might need to reduce oven temperature or cover the loaf loosely with foil during the last part of baking to prevent burning. The smell wafting through your kitchen should be a good guide: caramelized sugars, spices, and baking chocolate are some of the most comforting aromas you'll ever experience.

One of the most satisfying aspects of baking cinnamon swirl, babka, and chocolate loaves is the way they invite sharing. Whether it's sliced up for breakfast, served with coffee on a chilly morning, or wrapped up as a homemade gift, these breads bring joy straight from your oven to your family and friends. Plus, they store beautifully; tightly wrapped and refrigerated, they can safely last several days— and you can even freeze slices for longer enjoyment.

For beginners, it's easy to feel overwhelmed by the idea of these layered doughs and fillings, but remember each step builds on the previous ones you've already mastered. Don't rush through kneading or skipping proofing times just to get it done faster. Each minute spent nurturing your dough will shine through in the final loaf's texture and flavor. Enjoy the process of rolling out your dough, spreading your filling, and creating shapes—it's as much a moment of creativity as it is of science.

In the end, cinnamon swirl, babka, and chocolate loaves remind us what baking's all about: a little effort, some patience, and a lot of love can transform simple ingredients into something special. Once you're comfortable with these recipes and techniques, you'll find yourself excited to experiment with new fillings, spices, and variations. These loaves are invitations to make bread baking your own and share a slice of warmth with those around you.

Holiday Panettone and Stollen

As we continue exploring enriched, sweet, and festive breads, it's impossible to overlook two of the crown jewels of holiday baking: panettone and stollen. These beloved traditional loaves aren't just delicious; they carry rich histories and bring warmth and cheer to the holiday table. Perfect for novice bakers ready to venture into more involved projects, panettone and stollen blend sweet doughs, rich flavors, and aromatic spices in ways that reward patience and care with stunning results.

Panettone is a tall, dome-shaped Italian bread that originated in Milan and is now synonymous with Christmas festivities worldwide. Its light, fluffy crumb and complex flavor come from a highly enriched dough, often made with butter, eggs, sugar, and a generous mix of dried fruits like raisins, candied orange peel, and citron. Making panettone is sometimes seen as a challenge due to its lengthy fermentation process and the delicate gluten structure needed to hold its lofty dome shape. But with a bit of guidance and attention, even beginners can achieve success with this iconic bread.

To make panettone, it's important to start with a very good yeast activation and allow ample time for the dough to rise in stages. Unlike quick breads or simpler yeast loaves, panettone dough typically goes through multiple fermentations that develop flavor and the unique airy texture. The inclusion of eggs and butter makes this dough feel almost like a cake batter at first, but patient kneading and gentle folding help create the characteristic spongy network inside. A handy tip is to use a stand mixer or vigorous hand kneading to develop gluten without tearing the dough's delicate structure.

Once formed, the dough is usually placed in a tall paper mold, which holds its shape during the final rise and baking. This mold is essential and easy to find online or in specialty baking shops. Don't skip this step, as the paper mold allows your panettone to bake evenly and maintain its iconic silhouette. The aroma that fills your kitchen while it bakes is nothing short of festive magic—a mix of warm butter, citrus, and sweet dough that truly heralds the holidays.

On the other hand, stollen is the quintessential German holiday bread, dense and rich, studded with dried fruits, nuts, and marzipan, and finished with a generous dusting of powdered sugar. Stollen's origins trace back centuries, and traditionally, it was baked as a symbolic representation of the baby Jesus wrapped in swaddling clothes. This history might encourage slower, more mindful baking—it's as much about the ritual as the final product.

Like panettone, stollen dough is enriched with butter and sweetened with sugar. It's slightly denser and more bread-like, making it easier to handle during shaping. The inclusion of marzipan—the sweet almond paste—is a highlight for many and adds a creamy texture and nutty richness to every bite. If you're new to stollen baking, don't be intimidated by the enrichment and shaping process; the dough responds well to gentle kneading, and adding the fruit and nuts toward the end protects their texture and flavor.

One of the joys of baking stollen comes with its long lifespan. Unlike lighter breads, stollen actually improves in flavor if allowed to rest for a few days after baking. Wrapping it well and letting it sit in a cool place lets all the spices, dried fruits, and nuts meld beautifully, making each slice buttery, moist, and flavorful. This means you can bake your stollen in advance of the holidays and actually get better results by doing so—a real advantage for the busy home baker.

Both panettone and stollen benefit from using high-quality dried fruits and nuts. If possible, soak the raisins or fruit mix in warm water, rum, or brandy for an hour or even overnight. This not only plumps the fruit but also infuses your bread with subtle hints of that soaking liquid's flavor. Be sparing with alcohol if baking for children or those who avoid it, but a bit of fruit juice or even brewed tea can do the trick to enhance moisture and taste.

Timing is another piece of the puzzle. These breads are not quick projects—they demand multiple rising periods, sometimes upwards of 8 to 12 hours in total, spread over fermentation and proofing stages. This might feel overwhelming at first, but organizing your schedule with overnight rises or starting early in the day keeps the workload manageable. Plus, the reward of pulling a golden, aromatic panettone or stollen from your oven after all that waiting is more than worth it.

A tempting shortcut you might notice in some recipes is the use of commercial yeast to speed things up, but don't discount the flavor depth gained from longer fermentations, even when using yeast. If you'd like, you can explore a natural yeast starter for panettone to deepen those flavors even further, though this can be a more advanced step you tackle after mastering your first loaf.

When it comes to shaping, panettone's tall, domed form means it's important to handle the dough carefully so you don't deflate the air you've worked hard to develop. After the final rise, a simple time-tested trick is to insert a skewer or wooden dowel lengthwise to prevent the dome from collapsing as it cools. Stollen, however, is shaped like a traditional loaf folded over the marzipan and fruit, creating that signature oval, slightly flattened shape. This is easier than you might expect, involving gently stretching the dough and folding it over a log of marzipan before baking.

Finishing touches are crucial. Your baked panettone will often be brushed with a sugar glaze or light butter coating after baking to add shine and keep it moist. Stollen's signature look comes from a thick coat of butter brushed on immediately when it's out of the oven, followed by a heavy sprinkling of powdered sugar—almost like a snowy blanket. This layer not only tastes wonderful but helps seal in moisture, so don't skimp on it.

Both breads also lend themselves beautifully to variations. You can experiment by swapping candied citrus for cherries or cranberries in panettone, or add different nuts like pecans or walnuts in stollen. Some bakers even add spices like cinnamon or cardamom to the dough to create personalized, cozy holiday flavors. Keep in mind that while these additions offer fun customization, going too wild with the mix-ins can overwhelm the dough's rise and structure, so balance is key.

Once baked, these festive breads are best served sliced thick with some butter or alongside coffee and tea. Panettone, with its light airiness and sweet, citrusy notes, is wonderful toasted lightly the next day. Stollen's richness pairs perfectly with sharp cheeses or as a stand-alone treat with a dusting of extra powdered sugar. Both make excellent gifts—the thoughtful homemade touch is always memorable during the holiday season.

Starting your journey with holiday panettone and stollen transforms simple kitchen ingredients into storied works of edible art. While they take time and patience, these loaves reward every step with joyous aromas, beautiful presentation, and flavors that echo holiday traditions that span centuries. Embarking on these projects brings not only skill-building but also the pleasure of connecting with baking traditions that uplift family gatherings and holiday celebrations alike.

So pull out your mixing bowls, get comfortable with your yeast, and don't fear the challenge. Every expert was once a beginner who took the first spirited turn mixing dough. With each fold, rise, and bake, you're adding to a rich lineage of festive baking that celebrates warmth, community, and the delicious rewards of bread made with care.

Chapter 7
Rolls, Buns, and Bagels

Now that you've mastered the essentials of bread baking, it's time to dive into the world of rolls, buns, and bagels—each offering a unique texture and flavor that elevate any meal or snack. These breads may seem small, but they require attention to shaping and proofing to get that perfect rise and chewiness, whether you're aiming for soft, pillowy dinner rolls or the dense, slightly chewy bite of a classic bagel. Pay close attention to dough hydration and timing, as these factors make all the difference between a crust that's just right and one that's either too tough or too soft. And don't worry if the first batch isn't perfect; by practicing these versatile shapes, you'll gain confidence and soon find yourself experimenting with toppings, fillings, and even creative twists on traditional recipes. This chapter will guide you through those foundational techniques so your rolls, buns, and bagels turn out bakery-worthy every time.

Dinner Rolls, Parker House, and Pull-Apart Breads

When it comes to comfort breads, few things match the simple pleasure of warm dinner rolls fresh out of the oven.

These bite-sized treasures aren't just appetizers; they're the stars of family dinners, perfect for soaking up gravy or slathering with butter. If you're new to bread baking, dinner rolls offer a manageable way to build your skills without feeling overwhelmed by complex shaping or long fermentation times. They strike a wonderful balance between soft crumb and tender crust, making them incredibly inviting to novice bakers.

Dinner rolls come in many shapes and sizes—from classic round rolls to more elaborate knots and twists—but the unifying theme is their soft, pillowy texture. Achieving this involves a well-enriched dough, often incorporating milk, butter, and sometimes eggs, which tenderize the gluten strands and help the rolls keep their moisture. Unlike lean breads that emphasize crusty exteriors and chewy insides, these rolls are designed for softness and subtle sweetness, encouraging you to perfect gentle handling of dough.

One of the most iconic dinner roll styles is the Parker House roll, named after the Parker House Hotel in Boston where it was first made famous in the 1870s. These rolls are known for their distinctive shape—flattened ovals folded over before baking, resulting in a soft, buttery pull-apart texture. Their buttery richness and slightly crisp edges make them unforgettable. The technique behind Parker House rolls is straightforward, making them an ideal project to familiarize yourself with the nuances of shaping and proofing enriched doughs.

Getting these rolls just right hinges on a few essential steps. After your dough has risen, divide it into equal portions and gently flatten each piece before folding it in half to form the signature crescent shape. The rolls are then placed close together in the pan so they bake as a connected batch, which encourages them to rise up rather than outward. This closeness creates tender sides that are soft to the touch and wonderfully pull-apart. The dough itself should be silky and slightly sticky but still manageable; this feel signals that you've built enough gluten and hydrated the flour properly.

Pull-apart breads take the idea of connected rolls even further by arranging small pieces of dough tightly in a pan, which encourages them to rise and fuse together. These breads often come in sweet or savory variations and create an interactive eating experience, where each portion can be torn off by hand. It's a format that both young bakers and families appreciate for its casual, hands-on nature. With pull-apart breads, you can experiment by incorporating flavors like garlic and herb butter or cinnamon sugar infusions just before baking, opening the door to endless customization while sticking to a beginner-friendly process.

One of the great advantages of focusing on dinner rolls, Parker House, and pull-apart breads is their forgiving nature. Because the loaves are relatively small and baked close together, minor imperfections in shaping or proofing won't destroy the final product. This takes much of the pressure off and encourages a learning mindset, where you can see progress loaf by loaf. Plus, their shorter baking times mean you get delicious results quickly—perfect for maintaining momentum in your baking journey.

For novice bakers worried about timing, planning, or proofing, these rolls offer a perfect training ground. You don't have to worry about slow, cold fermentation or complicated scoring techniques here. Instead, your focus can rest on mastering dough feel, hydration, consistency in dividing, and a basic understanding of yeast fermentation. Watching the rolls rise and transform during their final proof is a great visual learning cue, linking your hands-on efforts to the science of fermentation you've encountered in earlier chapters.

Texture is another rewarding area to explore with these breads. The rich dough creates a crumb that's soft and tender, but also resilient enough to hold its shape without crumbling. This calls for just the right amount of kneading or stretch-and-folds to develop the gluten without toughening the dough. Many beginner bakers find this balance tricky at first, but dinner rolls give clear, repeatable feedback in their finished texture, helping you develop intuition. When you bite into a well-made Parker House roll or pull-apart loaf, you can literally taste your growing skill.

Beyond technique, baking these breads nurtures confidence and joy in the kitchen. There's something deeply satisfying about making small, perfect portions of bread that serve as the foundation for great meals and happy gatherings. Whether it's a family supper, holiday feast, or casual brunch, these rolls carry the warmth of tradition. They have a way of bringing people together, inviting sharing and savoring, which connects baking to culture and comfort in a special way.

As you progress, incorporating flavored butters or glazes like honey butter or herbed garlic oil becomes a natural next step. These simple additions don't complicate the process but elevate the breads' sensory appeal. Learning how to brush your rolls with melted butter right out of the oven is an easy yet transformative touch that adds shine, richness, and a tender crust. It's small rituals like this that make bread baking feel less like work and more like a craft worth loving.

Remember, the dough for these enriched breads is slightly stickier than simple lean doughs, and it can take some practice to handle it confidently. Use lightly floured hands and surfaces but avoid drying the dough out. Let your senses guide you: the dough should stretch smoothly without tearing and hold a soft shape rather than collapsing. As you gain experience, you'll start to notice subtle differences in dough feel, which inform your timing and technique for next time.

For those who want to step beyond the basics, try layering your pull-apart bread dough with slivers of cheese, herbs, or even small bits of cooked bacon before arranging it in the pan. These variations deepen flavor and build in exciting textures, while still keeping the overall technique approachable. Because the dough is divided into many small pieces, you get lots of opportunities to be creative and tailor each batch to your mood or meal.

Finally, the warm aroma and golden glow that fill your kitchen while baking dinner rolls or Parker House rolls add to the sensory pleasures of bread making. This sensory feedback isn't just comforting; it helps you develop a connection to the process that keeps you coming back for more. The relatively quick turnaround on these breads encourages a healthy rhythm of practice and reward, essential for building lasting baking habits.

In short, dinner rolls, Parker House rolls, and pull-apart breads form a welcoming and practical gateway into the world of bread baking. They teach fundamental skills wrapped in flavors and textures that comfort and delight. As you bake these breads, you also bake confidence, one soft roll at a time.

Burger Buns, Hot-Dog Buns, and Sliders

When it comes to burger buns, hot-dog buns, and sliders, these little breads play an outsized role in the eating experience. They're not just a vessel for meat and toppings—they're the foundation that holds everything together and enhances the flavors and textures of your sandwiches. Mastering these buns at home can transform a simple meal into something memorable. As a novice baker, you don't need to worry about complicated techniques to get great results. These buns typically require enriched doughs—that means dough enriched with fats like butter or oil, sometimes milk or eggs—which tenderize the crumb and add a faint sweetness. The result is soft, pillowy buns that still have enough structure to hold your fillings without falling apart.

Starting with burger buns, the classic American version is soft, slightly sweet, and round, with a smooth, shiny top. This shine usually comes from an egg wash applied before baking, which also adds color and a little gloss to make the buns look irresistible. These buns should have a tight, tender crumb that's sturdy enough for juicy burger patties and all your favorite toppings—from cheese to pickles to sauces. When shaping the rolls, aim for uniform size so they bake evenly and look professional. You'll notice that the dough is often a little sticky because of the milk and butter, but don't be tempted to add too much extra flour. Once you get the hang of shaping and proofing, the transformation in your homemade burgers will be noticeable.

Hot-dog buns have a longer, more elongated shape compared to burger buns. This shape is important because it cradles the hot dog or sausage snugly. The dough composition often resembles that of burger buns but tends to be lighter and more delicate. The secret to perfect hot-dog buns lies in shaping and scoring. Unlike burger buns, many hot-dog buns have a slit along the top or side before baking—this allows the bun to open just enough to hold the hot dog and toppings without tearing. Even if you don't score your buns, taking care with shaping helps maintain the right structure. It also helps if you proof the dough to a good height so the buns don't end up too dense or flat. The texture should be soft but resilient enough to withstand being squeezed and stacked with your favorite condiments.

Sliders, the mini versions of burgers, are growing in popularity and demand their own particular approach to buns. Because sliders rely heavily on the bun for their presentation, the buns need to be small, soft, and a bit sweet, but still sturdy enough to handle finger food handling. If you've experimented with dinner rolls, you'll find that slider buns often use a similar dough enriched with butter and sometimes a touch of sugar or honey. A slight sheen from an egg wash makes these buns look professional and inviting. When baking a batch of sliders, consider placing them close together on a baking sheet; this modest crowding encourages the buns to rise up tall with soft sides, creating that signature pull-apart quality perfect for serving several guests.

One tip for all three types of buns is to allow enough time for proper proofing. Under-proofed dough won't rise enough, leading to buns that are tight and tough. Over-proofed dough, on the other hand, can lead to flattening during baking or a crumb that's too open and crumbly. Finding just the right balance comes with practice, but as a guideline, proof until the dough roughly doubles and springs back slowly when poked gently. Remember that enriched doughs tend to proof faster because of the added sugars and fats, so keep an eye on your buns while they're rising.

The enriched doughs in these buns also want a tender crumb with a bit of elasticity—this helps the bun stretch a little as you bite through it, especially important for burgers loaded with toppings or hot dogs with plenty of mustard and relish. Balancing tenderness and structure means mixing your dough well but not over-kneading. A slightly tacky dough feels right, and incorporating proper gluten development ensures you won't end up with crumbly or flat buns. A simple test is to stretch a small piece of dough: if it stretches thin without tearing easily, the gluten is well developed.

When it comes to baking, temperature and timing play a critical role. Buns baked at an oven temperature around 375°F to 400°F create a browned, flavorful crust without drying out the soft crumb inside. Too hot, and you risk an overly thick crust or uneven baking; too cool, and the bun might remain pale and lack that signature color and texture. Check your buns frequently and rotate pans if needed to achieve uniform baking. You'll learn to sniff out the sweet smell of freshly baked bread that signals when to pull buns from the oven, a moment full of anticipation and reward.

As a beginner, something that helps immensely is preparing your dough the night before and refrigerating it. This cold fermentation slows down yeast activity, allowing the dough to develop more flavor and often making shaping easier because the dough firms up in the fridge. The next day, you can shape your buns right out of the fridge and let them warm up and finish proofing before baking. This approach can save time on busy days and helps build confidence with gentle dough handling.

While these buns are fairly simple to make, don't overlook the fun of customizing. Adding sesame seeds to burger buns, using poppy seeds on hot-dog buns, or brushing sliders with garlic butter after baking brings extra layers of flavor and aroma. These small touches make homemade buns stand out and also encourage you to keep baking more often. The rewards aren't just limited to taste—they build pride and joy in your kitchen achievements.

If you're worried about texture or crumb in your buns being too dense, chances are it's a proofing or shaping issue rather than a complicated recipe problem. Many beginners think they should add more flour if the dough is sticky, but that often results in tighter crumb and dryness. Instead, focus on the feel of the dough, proper kneading, and gently shaping to keep air bubbles while maintaining dough consistency. It's a balance, but one that becomes natural with practice.

Finally, storing your buns properly preserves their softness and freshness longer. Wrap cooled buns in plastic or keep them in an airtight container at room temperature if you'll consume them within a couple of days. For longer storage, freeze your buns either individually wrapped or in groups. When ready to use, a quick zap in the microwave wrapped in a damp paper towel or a toasting session revives their softness and warmth nicely. Homemade buns are worth the effort because no store-bought substitute can match the taste and texture of freshly baked bread under your own hands.

Whether you're biting into a juicy burger, a loaded hot dog, or popping slider sandwiches at your next get-together, freshly baked buns anchor the whole experience.

Getting comfortable with enriched doughs, gentle shaping, and perfect proofing times might seem daunting at first, but with each loaf, you're learning important fundamentals that transfer to countless recipes down the road. Most importantly, the joy you'll feel when biting into the bun you made yourself is unmatched—and that's why this chapter matters as much as any.

NY-Style Bagels and Pretzel Buns

Few things capture the essence of New York City baking quite like its iconic bagels. NY-style bagels have a distinct character, which sets them apart from many other bagel variations around the world. The defining qualities are a shiny, chewy crust and a dense, slightly doughy interior that holds up beautifully whether toasted or eaten fresh. Mastering these bagels at home can seem a bit daunting at first, but with patience and some technique, you'll find they're incredibly rewarding.

What makes a New York bagel so unique? It starts with the dough itself—a high-gluten flour is a must to build that signature chewiness. Most recipes call for bread flour due to its higher protein content, which encourages a strong gluten network. This allows the bagel to maintain its structure when boiled and baked. The dough is usually slightly sweetened, often with malt syrup or honey, which not only feeds the yeast but also adds subtle flavor and encourages browning during baking.

The process of boiling before baking is key to achieving the bagel's crust. Boiling gelatinizes the starches on the dough's surface, creating that beautiful glossy skin you associate with bagels. The boiling water sometimes includes a bit of barley malt syrup or baking soda, which affects the final color and texture. Barley malt gives a deep golden hue and a slightly tangy taste, while baking soda alkalizes the water and promotes browning. Timing in the boil is critical: bagels typically boil for 30 to 60 seconds on each side. Any longer, and they can become gummy; shorter, and the crust won't develop properly.

After boiling, the bagels go straight into a hot oven for baking. A steamy environment in the first few minutes helps develop a nice crust. When you bake at the right temperature, a balance is struck between the crunchy exterior and a tender crumb inside. Once cooled, the bagels are ready for slicing—whether for sandwiches or toasting with your favorite spreads.

For beginners, shaping bagels might seem fiddly, but it's really all about practice. The traditional method involves rolling the dough into a log, then joining the ends to form a ring. Some folks prefer rolling the dough into a ball and poking a hole through the center, gently stretching it to the perfect size. Remember, the hole will shrink during boiling and baking, so aim for a noticeably large opening before cooking. Your bagels will puff up and shrink the hole, so don't worry if it looks too big initially.

Beyond the classic bagel, New York has also inspired a beloved fusion: the pretzel bun. If you're familiar with German pretzels, you might already appreciate their chewy skin and rich flavor from an alkaline bath before baking. Pretzel buns borrow this characteristic treatment but with a soft, sandwich-friendly shape. They're a perfect, satisfying alternative to common burger buns or sandwich rolls.

Pretzel buns involve dipping shaped dough into a baking soda solution before baking. This quick dip alters the pH of the surface, facilitating Maillard browning, which gives pretzels their deep brown color and mouthwatering, slightly crisp crust. Inside, the crumb should stay soft and airy enough for sandwiches but maintain a slight chew from the alkaline wash. The combination of rich, browned crust and pillowy interior makes these buns incredibly versatile.

If you want to experiment, an easy way to tie the bagel and pretzel worlds together is by trying pretzel-style bagels. These hybrids bring the traditional bagel's dense crumb together with the pretzel's dark, crackly crust from the baking soda bath. It's a fun twist if you love both and want a fresh take that stands out. Just keep in mind the boiling step usually gets replaced by the baking soda dunk for pretzel treatments.

Both NY-style bagels and pretzel buns benefit greatly from attention to dough hydration and fermentation timing. Bagel doughs tend to be a bit stiffer than other breads, around 50-55% hydration. This firmness helps maintain shape during the boiling and baking process. Overly wet dough can spill or lose structure, so keep measurements precise. On the other hand, pretzel buns sometimes enjoy slightly higher hydration—55-60%—to maintain softness inside while still developing a chewy crust. Keeping your dough covered and relaxed during bulk fermentation is vital to prevent a dry skin from forming; it also supports a better rise.

Yeast activity is another factor you'll want to watch carefully. Because bagels are boiled, the interior isn't baked at a very high temperature for very long, so it's important the dough has risen fully before shaping. Underproofed bagels could lead to overly dense textures, while overproofed ones might lose their shape during boiling. For pretzel buns, proofing until doubled in size usually works well, allowing a nice oven spring and open crumb without collapsing under the weight of the alkaline bath treatment.

When it comes to toppings, the possibilities open up further. NY bagels are famously adorned with everything from poppy and sesame seeds to salt or "everything" seasoning blends. These toppings add crunch and flavor contrast to the chewiness beneath. Some bakers suggest adding toppings after boiling but before baking, which helps them stick and toast beautifully during the bake. If you prefer a cleaner bagel look, enjoy them plain or with a simple egg wash for extra shine.

Pretzel buns often sport a sprinkling of coarse salt on top, which enhances their savory appeal and crust texture. For a different spin, try brushing butter over buns as they come out of the oven—this adds moisture and a lovely sheen. These little touches elevate your homemade rolls to bakery-level treats anyone would be thrilled to serve.

If you're aiming to speed up your baking routine, prepare your bagel or pretzel dough in advance. Both doughs freeze well, so consider making batches to keep on hand for whenever you're ready. Thaw dough completely and give it a short rest to warm up before shaping and fermenting again slightly—a trick that helps reboot the yeast and gluten.

Finally, remember that tasting and adjusting are part of the journey. Every kitchen is different—water chemistry, flour brands, and even oven types influence the final product. Take notes on what works, and don't hesitate to tweak hydration, boiling times, or baking temperatures based on your experience. Baking NY-style bagels and pretzel buns is equal parts science and art, and each batch teaches you something new.

Embracing these culinary staples from New York means enjoying not only their iconic flavor and texture but also the baking process itself. Once you've nailed your first batch, you'll see just how accessible these classic rolls and bagels really are. Plus, fresh homemade bagels or pretzel buns save you trips to the store and deliver unbeatable satisfaction with every bite.

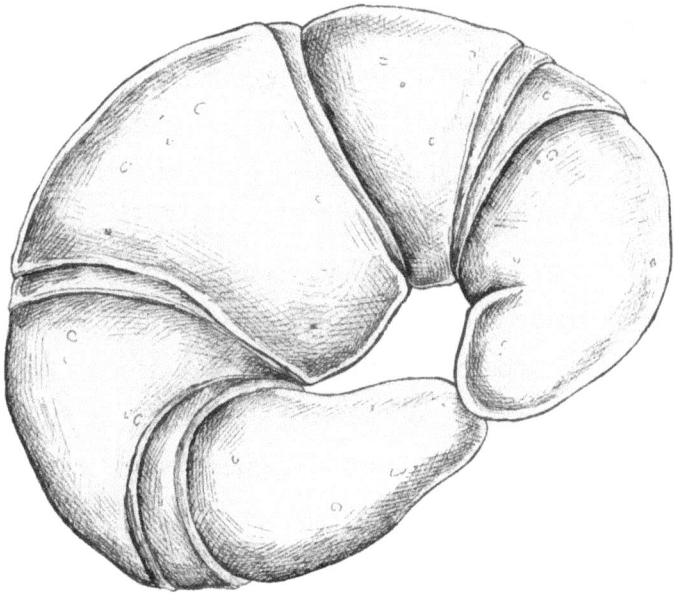

Chapter 8
Flatbreads and Everyday Staples

———— »»»› ‹‹‹« ————

Transitioning from loaves that fill your kitchen with hearty aromas, let's explore flatbreads and other everyday staples that bring versatility and speed to your baking repertoire. These breads, from the pillowy softness of pita to the golden crisp of tortillas, often require less rising time and fewer ingredients, making them perfect for busy days or last-minute meals. Mastering these flatbreads opens doors to countless culinary possibilities, whether it's layering naan in a curry feast, stacking chapati for a cozy dinner, or crafting your own pizza crusts that serve as the perfect canvas for toppings. The beauty lies not just in their simplicity, but also in their ability to connect you with global traditions—all achievable in your home kitchen with confidence and care.

Pita, Naan, and Chapati

Flatbreads hold a special place in many cultures, and mastering a few basic types can really expand your bread-baking repertoire. Let's dive into three beloved, everyday flatbreads: pita, naan, and chapati. Each brings its own unique flavor, texture, and method to the table, yet they share a common thread of simplicity and versatility that makes them great for home bakers who want to explore beyond the classic loaf.

Pita is widely recognized for its iconic pocket, making it an excellent choice for stuffing with your favorite fillings. Achieving that pocket relies on a combination of high heat and steam that causes the dough to puff up quickly during baking, separating the layers and creating a hollow interior. The dough itself usually has simple ingredients: flour, water, yeast, salt, and sometimes a bit of olive oil. What's wonderful about pita is how approachable it is. The process emphasizes high hydration and short fermentation times, which help produce a soft yet chewy bread. Pita's quick rise can encourage beginners to observe firsthand how yeast activity transforms dough within just an hour or two. Once baked, you can serve pita warm from the oven with dips, grilled veggies, meats, or turn them into sandwich pockets. Even leftovers make great toasters for a quick snack.

Naan, on the other hand, is traditionally found in Indian and Central Asian cuisines and carries a richer and softer profile compared to most basic flatbreads. Its dough typically includes yogurt and sometimes milk or eggs, imparting a tender crumb and a slight tang that sets naan apart. These additions not only enrich the bread but also help it hold moisture, making naan wonderfully soft even after cooling. Traditional naan is cooked in a tandoor oven, which reaches blistering temperatures and cooks the bread in minutes, producing characteristic charring and a smoky flavor. At home, recreating this effect means using a very hot skillet or oven, and sometimes finishing the bread under a broiler to get those signature charred spots. Though it sounds intimidating, it's entirely doable even on a modest stove. The dough's elasticity makes it perfect for rolling out to varying thicknesses, whether you prefer a thicker, chewier naan or a thinner, breadier version more like a wrap.

Chapati, sometimes called roti, differs quite a bit from both pita and naan with its simplicity shining through. It's an unleavened bread, meaning it doesn't use yeast or any leavening agent, relying solely on whole wheat flour and water. The dough is supple, and after resting briefly, it's rolled out thin into discs and cooked on a hot griddle or cast-iron skillet. Chapati is celebrated for its light, pliable texture and subtle whole grain flavor. Because the dough is unleavened, patience during rolling and cooking is key to achieving that puffed, tender bread. Many home bakers find chapati surprisingly quick to pull together, with the bonus that it pairs beautifully with vegetable curries, grilled meats, and even breakfast spreads.

Understanding these flatbreads' basic techniques is crucial before diving into recipes. For pita, focus on developing a smooth, soft dough with enough hydration to create the steam needed in the oven. The dough is shaped into rounds and allowed a short final rise—about 30 minutes—before baking on a hot stone or tray. Timing the bake right is important; too long and the pockets can collapse, too short and the bread won't puff up properly. To guarantee success, preheat your oven to its maximum setting and consider adding a pan of water at the bottom to increase humidity. It's worth experimenting with oven temperature and baking times to find what works best with your equipment.

When working with naan dough, mix and knead until the dough feels soft and silky but still holds its shape. Letting it ferment for an hour or two at room temperature accelerates flavor development, but it's not as critical as with yeast breads because of the yogurt's acidity. Rolling the dough balls out evenly ensures they cook consistently on the skillet. Cooking naan requires patience and attention— medium-high heat lets the dough cook through without burning, while flipping multiple times creates the perfect blistered char. Don't forget to brush the cooked bread with melted butter or ghee; this small step takes naan from simply good to indulgently delicious.

Chapati dough, by contrast, demands a deft hand. The flour-to-water ratio can vary based on the brand of whole wheat flour you use. Allowing the dough to rest after kneading, even for just 20 to 30 minutes, hydrates the flour fully and makes rolling easier. When rolling chapatis, use just enough pressure to stretch the dough without tearing it, keeping the discs as round and thin as possible. Cooking chapati on a hot, dry skillet requires quick, attentive flipping. A perfect chapati puffs up as steam escapes, giving it a light interior and tender bite. If puffing doesn't happen right away, don't worry—that might be due to uneven rolling or skillet temperature; continued practice will improve results.

One aspect that ties all three of these flatbreads together is their accessibility: the ingredients are pantry staples, and the techniques don't necessitate advanced tools or complicated equipment. For novice bakers, flatbreads like pita, naan, and chapati introduce important foundational skills such as managing hydration, shaping dough for specific textures, and controlling cooking temperatures to achieve the right crust and crumb.

It's also inspiring to recognize how these breads serve as everyday staples globally. They offer more than just sustenance—they provide a cultural connection and a reminder that simple dough can unite diverse tables. By practicing these recipes, you're not just baking bread; you're stepping into a timeless tradition of communal meals and shared stories.

For beginners looking for success, start small. Pick one—the pita's pocket, the naan's tender richness, or the chapati's rustic charm—and bake it several times, observing how the dough feels and behaves. Keep notes on temperature, timing, and texture during each trial. As your confidence grows, experiment with additions like garlic, herbs, or seeds to customize the flatbreads to your taste. Flatbreads offer incredible room for creativity and adaptation, and this flexibility encourages bakers of all levels to make them their own.

In the end, these flatbreads teach patience, observation, and an appreciation of humble ingredients transformed through simple, time-honored techniques. Whether your goal is to fill pita pockets with grilled chicken and salad, serve naan alongside spicy curries, or enjoy fresh chapati with butter and jam, mastering these breads will enrich your kitchen skills and provide a reliable, delicious foundation for countless meals.

Tortillas, Arepas, and English Muffins

When thinking about everyday staples that feel both comforting and incredibly versatile, tortillas, arepas, and English muffins stand out. These three flatbreads come from very different culinary traditions, yet each offers a warm, inviting canvas for countless meals. If you've worked through previous chapters mastering doughs and fermentation, these breads provide a satisfying pivot point: simpler in technique but rich in cultural texture and flavor. Plus, they make for perfect starters if you want quick breads without sacrificing the joy of homemade baking.

Tortillas, especially corn and flour varieties, have been a foundational bread in Mexican and Central American kitchens for centuries. They're deceptively simple: just a handful of ingredients—flour or masa harina, water, salt, and sometimes a fat like lard or oil. What really matters is the technique and the heat source when you cook them. Tortillas don't usually involve yeast or rising agents, setting them apart from many other breads, but that doesn't mean they're basic. Their thin, pliable structure demands precise mixing and rolling to avoid toughness. For a beginner baker, mastering tortillas is a lesson in patience and finesse, improving your feel for dough hydration and thickness.

The beauty of homemade tortillas is that you control every element, from the flour to the cooking time. Flour tortillas, with their soft and tender crumb, are excellent for wraps, quesadillas, or simply tearing off to scoop up savory stews. Corn tortillas have a firmer, earthier character, holding their shape better and offering a slight chew that many love. Learning to make both lets you explore the subtleties of corn nixtamalization—treated corn that transforms both flavor and texture—and wheat flour blending. If you're turning out tortillas for the first time, it's tempting to compare them to supermarket brands, but homemade always rises above in freshness and aroma.

Shifting gears, arepas come primarily from Venezuela and Colombia but have found fans worldwide thanks to their satisfying, approachable nature. Made from pre-cooked cornmeal—often referred to as masarepa—arepas are thicker than most tortillas and typically cooked on a griddle or fried. One of the most delightful things about arepas is how their interiors puff slightly when cooked, creating small air pockets that soak up spreads, cheeses, or stews. Though simple in ingredients, arepas introduce the home cook to a different kind of corn-based bread that strikes a nice balance between softness and just enough crunch on the outside.

Arepas don't demand fermentation, which means you can mix the dough and cook the bread within minutes, making them perfect for busy home kitchens. For beginners, working with masarepa encourages an understanding of cornmeal's water absorption, and the difference between raw and pre-cooked corn flours. As you get comfortable, you can adapt arepas by adding ingredients like cheese into the dough or creating fillings once they're cooked, turning them from a side into the star of your meal. Their mildly sweet corn flavor also means they adapt well to both savory and slightly sweet pairings.

English muffins, on the other hand, belong to a tradition rooted in yeast-leavened baking but are uniquely characterized by their signature nooks and crannies and griddle-baked surface. Unlike many breads baked in an oven, English muffins get their trademark texture from being cooked slowly on a hot griddle or skillet, resulting in a browned exterior with a chewy interior full of little pockets. These pockets don't just look pretty; they're perfect for holding melted butter, jam, or savory toppings, making English muffins a beloved breakfast staple across many households.

For new bakers, English muffins can feel a little more technical since they require yeast for a gentle rise and careful handling during shaping and cooking. However, once you nail the rhythm of mixing, proofing, and griddle-baking, they quickly become a rewarding project. The process teaches critical bread skills like controlling fermentation time and practicing consistent shaping—skills that tie back to earlier chapters but with a fresh twist. You'll also gain a better sense for cooking temperature since even slight overheating can burn the exterior before the dough cooks through.

One of the nice things about English muffins is their versatility. They can be served toasted with simple butter and jam or built into breakfast sandwiches with eggs, cheese, and bacon. Once you've tried the homemade version, with its complex flavor and chewy texture, it's hard to go back to store-bought. The satisfaction from transforming simple ingredients—flour, yeast, milk, and a little butter—into these golden, griddle-bound delights is remarkable.

When you combine making tortillas, arepas, and English muffins, you're gaining not only an array of staple breads but also an understanding of how different cultures approach flatbreads and everyday baking. Each recipe introduces a unique method: the quick-cooking, no-yeast simplicity of tortillas and arepas versus the yeast-leavened, pan-cooked technique of English muffins. With these breads, there's a sense of immediacy—tortillas and arepas come together fast, while English muffins require a bit more patience but are no less manageable for beginners.

It's common to feel a little intimidated when you see flatbreads labeled as "artisan" or "traditional," but these staples often rely on straightforward methods and modest ingredients. The key is focusing on dough consistency and cooking temperature, which influence texture and flavor as much as ingredient quality. For example, a tortilla that's rolled too thick won't fold nicely; an arepa that's too wet will crumble instead of form a crisp crust; and an English muffin cooked on a skillet that's too hot will brown on the outside without cooking properly inside.

If you're experimenting with these breads, try to embrace the tactile experience—press the masa-dough, feel when your tortilla dough is soft but not sticky, watch how the English muffins bubble and brown on the griddle. There's a rhythm in these processes that sharpens your instincts as a baker. Also, don't be discouraged by imperfect rounds or slight thickness variations. The beauty of these flatbreads is their rustic, handmade charm and the way they taste—each bite connecting you to centuries of tradition and simple, satisfying nourishment.

Beyond just the baking, these breads can change how you approach meals at home. Tortillas make everyday dinners feel like celebrations with tacos or wraps filled with fresh, seasonal produce and proteins. Arepas are a canvas for creativity, offering a handheld delight that can work with nearly any filling imaginable, from creamy avocados and cheeses to hearty beans and meats. English muffins transform breakfasts, turning morning routines into small moments of pleasure with perfectly toasted crumpets to hold jam or eggs. Learning them expands not only your baking skills but also your culinary repertoire and meal ideas.

In terms of storage and use, tortillas and arepas are best eaten fresh but can be warmed up easily on a dry skillet or in a microwave for a few seconds. English muffins can be split, toasted, and frozen for later use. Each has its place in your kitchen rhythm—quick fixes to accompany weeknight dinners or leisurely weekend breakfasts. The more you make these, the more you'll find little personal tweaks that make them uniquely yours: a pinch of seasoning in arepas, a splash of milk in your English muffin dough, or a perfectly thin tortilla roll-out that feels just right.

In closing, these breads invite you to think of baking not just as an exact science but as an enjoyable, sensory experience with plenty of room for exploration and personalization. Tortillas, arepas, and English muffins each offer a different way to build confidence with dough handling, perfect cooking techniques, and fresh, simple ingredients. Mastering these staples is also an open door to cultures and traditions, adding not just food skills but stories and flavors to your kitchen. Whether folded, filled, or split and toasted, they nourish both body and soul—ready to start that journey is truly rewarding.

Pizza Crusts: Thin, Thick, and Sourdough

Pizza crust is where the magic begins. It's the foundation that holds all those delicious toppings together, and depending on the style you're after, the crust itself can become the star of the show. Whether you prefer a paper-thin, crispy base, a soft and pillowy thick crust, or the tangy complexity of a sourdough, understanding how each crust works can transform your pizza game from good to unforgettable.

Starting with thin crusts, these are often prized for their crispness and light chew. The goal here is to achieve a delicate balance—a crust that's sturdy enough to support toppings but still crisp and almost crackly on the edges. The secret usually lies in a high hydration dough and sometimes a touch of oil for tenderness. Because thin crusts are stretched out so thin, they bake quickly, often in just minutes on a super-hot surface or stone. For home bakers, replicating that restaurant-level blistering heat can be challenging, but with a pizza stone or steel in a hot oven, it's totally doable. The thin crust reacts quickly to the heat, resulting in those lovely leopard spots of char and crisp edges that make every bite sing.

Contrasting this, thick crusts invite a completely different experience. They're soft and often bready, with a chewy interior and a golden, slightly crunchy exterior. Thick crusts are more forgiving in terms of handling and timing at home, making them a great candidate for novice bakers who want to build confidence. With more dough per pizza, the crumb structure becomes important. This type of dough usually contains a touch more yeast and sometimes a bit of sugar to encourage a nice rise and flavorful caramelization on the crust. Additionally, the proofing time is crucial—insufficient proofing will lead to a dense, doughy crust, while over-proofing can cause the crust to collapse. Think of thick crust pizza almost like mini loaves: airy pockets of crumb that provide contrast to saucy, cheesy toppings.

Then there's sourdough pizza crust, which has surged in popularity among home cooks and professional chefs alike. Working with sourdough starter to make pizza crust adds extra layers of flavor, complexity, and texture. The natural fermentation not only gives the dough a characteristic tang but also produces a better chew and a crust that holds up well to an abundance of toppings without becoming soggy. Sourdough crust benefits from longer fermentation and often cold proofing in the fridge, which helps develop those nuanced flavors and a more digestible crumb. If you've already dabbled in sourdough bread, this is a fantastic next step to put your starter to good use and explore the versatile world of naturally leavened flatbreads.

Each style of crust demands different attention to detail, especially with regard to dough handling. Thin crusts thrive on quick, confident stretching and minimal toppings to keep weight in check. If the dough is torn or too thick in spots, it won't crisp evenly. With thick crusts, volume and fermentation time become your best friends; you want that dough to be bubbly and airy so it bakes through fully without a gummy center. Sourdough crusts, meanwhile, require patience—a longer fermentation and often a bit of skill balancing hydration and starter maturity to get just the right balance between rise, chew, and flavor.

Flour choice can also subtly influence your pizza dough's texture. High-protein bread flour is often favored for its gluten strength, which supports good stretch and chew in both thin and thick crusts. Some bakers like to blend bread flour with a bit of all-purpose or even Italian Tipo 00 flour for that silky crumb structure prized in traditional Neapolitan-style thin crusts. If you prefer a chewier thick crust, sticking with straight bread flour usually works best. For sourdoughs, using bread flour or a blend including some whole wheat can add depth of flavor and a more rustic appeal, though it may require slight adjustments in hydration since whole grains absorb more water.

One of the biggest hurdles for beginners is mastering the dough stretch. Thin crust requires a delicate touch and confidence not to overwork or tear the dough. Using your hands and gravity, letting the dough gently stretch over time, is preferable to forcing it with a rolling pin, which compresses the gas bubbles and results in a denser crust. For thick crusts, the stretch is often gentler—you want to preserve as many bubbles as possible to keep the crumb light and springy once baked. If you're going sourdough, expect to spend extra time as the dough is generally stickier and less forgiving, but the payoff in flavor and texture makes that extra effort worthwhile.

Baking technique plays a starring role regardless of crust style. Thin crusts love intense, radiant heat for a short time. If your oven doesn't reach 500 degrees Fahrenheit, use a preheated pizza stone or steel to simulate those conditions. Bake quickly to get that golden-brown, charred effect without drying out the base. Thick crusts require a bit more time to ensure the dough cooks through, often at a slightly lower temperature than thin crusts. You can also experiment with par-baking the crust before adding toppings to avoid sogginess. Sourdough crust can benefit from a two-step bake as well: a hot initial bake to get the crust started, then finishing off slightly lower for even crumb cooking.

Texture is another major point of differentiation that affects topping selection and pizza style. Thin crusts, naturally, can't hold heavy, watery toppings well—less is often more here. Conversely, thick crust pizzas, like the Chicago-style deep dish or Sicilian squares, are built for luscious layers of sauce, cheese, and toppings. Their thick, doughy bases soak up flavors beautifully and provide a hearty mouthfeel. Sourdough crust pizza is often a versatile canvas, balancing crispness and chew, letting toppings shine while contributing its own complex, tangy notes.

For home bakers, experimenting with these three crust styles opens up a rich playground of baking. Start by mastering one—thin crust maybe—and focus on fine-tuning hydration and baking temperature. When that feels comfortable, branch out to thick crusts, paying special attention to fermentation and crumb structure. Incorporate sourdough last, so you can build on your knowledge of natural leavening and handling more hydrated, delicate dough.

No matter which crust you choose, baking is about patience and gentle curiosity. Sometimes your dough will need a little extra time to proof, or your oven may require some tweaking to reach optimal heat. Mistakes are part of the process, revealing what changes to make for the next bake. With every pizza tossed, rolled, or stretched, you're getting closer to the perfect homemade crust that suits your tastes and style.

Remember, pizza crust combines science with art. It's chemistry in the mixing bowl, fermentation tension play, and heat alchemy inside the oven. And best of all, it's a chance to share a labor of love, whether with a family dinner or a casual weekend treat. So embrace the journey, savor each bite, and enjoy creating your own signature pizzas one crust at a time.

Chapter 9
Gluten-Free Bread Baking

B aking gluten-free bread can feel like stepping into a whole new world, but it doesn't have to be daunting. Unlike traditional bread, gluten-free baking relies on a blend of flours and binders to mimic the texture and structure gluten usually provides, so understanding these ingredients is key for success. Patience matters here, as gluten-free doughs often behave differently during mixing and proofing, requiring gentle handling rather than vigorous kneading. With the right balance of moisture, leavening agents, and a bit of experimentation, you can create loaves that are light, tender, and flavorful — perfect for sandwiches or artisan-style breads. This chapter will guide you through the essentials of gluten-free flour choices and techniques, helping you build confidence to enjoy baking without gluten while still achieving satisfying results every time.

Gluten-Free Flour Basics

Switching from traditional wheat flour to gluten-free flours can feel like stepping into a whole new world. Unlike wheat, gluten-free flours don't have that natural protein structure that gives bread its elasticity and chew. That means your approach to flour — and baking in general — needs to adjust accordingly. But don't worry; once you understand the basics, you'll gain confidence and soon be whipping up gluten-free loaves that rival any traditional bread.

One of the trickiest things about gluten-free flours is that they don't behave the same way wheat flour does. Gluten forms a stretchy network that traps gas bubbles created during fermentation, letting bread rise and develop that airy crumb. Gluten-free flours lack this protein, so they usually produce denser, heavier bread if you rely on a single flour type. That's why almost all gluten-free bread recipes call for a blend of different flours and starches. Each component plays a role in mimicking gluten's structure—or at least compensating for its absence.

Popular gluten-free flours come from a variety of grains, nuts, and other plants, each with its own flavor, texture, and baking properties. Rice flour is a staple in many blends for its neutral taste and relatively fine texture. Tapioca starch is a magic ingredient for adding stretch and a pleasantly chewy crumb, while potato starch helps with moisture retention and softness. Almond flour adds richness and a subtle nutty flavor but doesn't contribute much structure, so it's often combined with others. Understanding what each flour or starch brings to the table helps you create better blends and results.

When you experiment with gluten-free flours, keep in mind that absorption rates vary quite a bit. Some flours soak up water quickly; others hardly do at all. For instance, brown rice flour absorbs more moisture than white rice flour, and bean-based flours like garbanzo flour hold water differently—and are richer in protein. This means measuring flour by weight rather than volume is crucial for consistency. Also, expect to tweak hydration levels in your dough or batter since stiffness and stickiness aren't reliable indicators for "just right" with gluten-free mixes.

Since gluten-free flours behave differently, many recipes rely on xanthan gum, guar gum, or psyllium husk powder to help hold the dough together and create that chewy texture bread lovers expect. These binders don't add flavor, but they act as stand-ins for gluten's gluey quality. Psyllium husk is particularly popular because it also improves moisture retention, leading to bread that stays softer—and fresher—longer. Don't be intimidated by these ingredients; think of them as helpful tools that make your gluten-free loaf possible.

Another important tip is to always sift or whisk your gluten-free flours and starches before mixing. This step prevents lumps and ensures an even distribution of ingredients, which is essential for good texture and consistent rising. Gluten-free doughs often start as a thick batter rather than a traditional elastic dough. As you mix, you'll see the dough will feel wetter and more delicate. Trying to knead gluten-free dough the same way you would wheat dough usually results in tearing and collapsing. Instead, gentle folding or simply stirring is the way to go.

Because gluten-free breads tend to be denser and crumbly, many home bakers find that baking in a loaf pan helps support the structure while baking, especially when you're starting out. A loaf pan gives the shape and helps hold everything together during the heat of the oven. Also, some gluten-free bread recipes do better with a longer proof time or slightly warmer temperature to encourage a fuller rise. However, too much proofing usually makes the dough collapse because the structure can't support itself indefinitely. Watching the dough closely rather than relying on a timer is often best.

The flavor profile of your gluten-free bread will also depend significantly on the flour blend you use. Some flours, like sorghum or millet, have a slightly sweet, nutty flavor, while bean flours can add an earthy note. Nut-based flours provide depth and richness but can make the loaf heavier. Blending several flours balances these characteristics and helps avoid overpowering or unpleasant aftertastes. Sources vary widely, so mix and match to find the combination you love most.

Storage is another area where gluten-free bread differs. It tends to dry out faster than wheat breads and can become crumbly if left uncovered. Wrapping your bread tightly in plastic wrap or storing it in an airtight container keeps moisture in. For longer-term storage, freezing slices or whole loaves is a great option; wrap well to avoid freezer burn. When you want to enjoy your bread again, simply thaw at room temperature or lightly toast it for a fresh-from-the-oven feel.

As you get more comfortable with gluten-free flour basics, you'll discover more tricks and adjustments. Each flour blend responds uniquely depending on humdity, altitude, and your oven's quirks. Keep tasting, testing, and learning. Pay attention to how your dough looks and feels at every step. Over time, patience and practice will turn into intuition—and the loaves you create will grow more beautiful, flavorful, and satisfying with every batch.

Remember that gluten-free bread baking is as much about creativity as following rules. Being open to blending flours, adjusting hydration, and experimenting with binders frees you from frustration. Your goal is a loaf that tastes great and feels good in your hands—not a carbon copy of traditional wheat bread. With these flour basics in your toolkit, you're ready to move forward with confidence and excitement, ready to try your hand at the delicious recipes that follow.

No-Knead Gluten-Free Sandwich Loaf

Baking gluten-free bread can feel like stepping into a new world, especially if you're used to the stretch and pull of traditional wheat doughs. But here's the good news: you don't need to knead gluten-free dough to get a soft, tender sandwich loaf that holds together just right. No-knead gluten-free breads rely on hydration, gentle mixing, and patience to develop structure instead of muscle power. This method is a game changer for home bakers looking for simplicity without sacrificing flavor or texture.

The key to a successful no-knead gluten-free sandwich loaf starts with a good blend of flours and starches. A mixture often includes rice flour, tapioca starch, and sometimes other flours like sorghum or millet to balance flavor and crumb. Each flour brings something unique: rice flour adds body, tapioca starch lends chewiness and elasticity, and other flours contribute depth and complexity. You won't find any wheat or traditional gluten-containing flours here, so the loaf depends on clever chemistry and hydration to get fluffy and tender.

When mixing your ingredients, simplicity is crucial. Combine your dry ingredients—including gluten-free flour blend, xanthan gum or guar gum for binding, yeast for rising, salt, and sometimes a touch of sugar or honey to feed the yeast. Then, add liquids like warm water, oil, and eggs or egg substitute. The batter-like dough will be wetter and looser than what you're used to with wheat dough, more like a thick pancake batter than a kneadable dough ball. This moisture level is essential, giving the loaf a moist crumb and a tender crust.

One of the best parts about the no-knead gluten-free approach is letting the dough do the work over time. After a brief but firm stir to combine everything, the batter rests for a long fermentation—usually between 8 to 12 hours at room temperature. This slow rise lets the yeast gently carbonize the dough, creating bubbles you can't quite see but will feel in the loaf's lift and softness. It's also a perfect hands-off period to plan the rest of your baking day, no rush or fuss required.

Before baking, this loaf benefits from a quick shape in a loaf pan. Some might worry about working with sticky dough, but the secret is lightly oiling your hands and the pan. Once transferred, give the dough a final rest to puff up— about 45 minutes to an hour is ideal. This resting time lets tiny pockets of gas grow and ensures your bread rises evenly in the oven. Don't be tempted to press the dough down too much here; be gentle and let the dough bloom in the warmth.

Baking is straightforward, too. A moderate oven temperature, typically around 350°F (175°C), works well for this loaf. It's about slow, steady baking to let heat penetrate through the moist dough and set the crumb without drying it out. Covering the loaf with foil partway through baking can help prevent overly browned tops, but removing the foil in the last 10 minutes will give a nice golden crust. Unlike traditional bread, gluten-free crusts tend to be thinner and softer, which works perfectly for sandwich bread—you want something tender to bite into rather than a thick chewy crust.

Once out of the oven, resist the urge to cut too soon. Gluten-free breads continue to set and moisten a bit as they cool. Patience at this stage is rewarded with slices that hold together without crumbling apart. When cooled completely, wrapping the loaf tightly or storing it in an airtight container is key to maintain moisture. Gluten-free breads dry out faster, so freezing slices individually is a great way to keep your loaf fresh for longer.

This no-knead method also opens the door to customization. You can add herbs, seeds, or nuts to the batter for extra flavor and texture. Chopped olives, garlic powder, or dried cranberries can make your sandwich loaf uniquely yours without complicating the process. With gentle additions like these, your bread goes from simple and reliable to irresistibly tasty.

For home bakers just beginning their gluten-free journey, this loaf offers both encouragement and success. Baking gluten-free bread doesn't have to feel overwhelming or require complicated equipment. Starting with a no-knead recipe builds confidence and helps you appreciate how ingredients interact without the fuss of kneading sticky dough. Each loaf teaches a little more about hydration, rising times, and the subtle magic of gluten-free baking chemistry.

Expect this loaf to be a versatile companion in your kitchen—perfect for sandwiches, toast, or even French toast on the weekend. Its soft crumb and mild flavor make it friendly to all kinds of toppings and fillings, from peanut butter to fresh tomatoes and basil. You're creating more than just bread; you're making an everyday staple that supports your gluten-free lifestyle with ease and taste.

Remember, no-knead gluten-free bread is forgiving. Small differences in temperature, flour brands, or humidity can affect the rise and texture. Don't be discouraged if your first loaf isn't perfect; learning to bake gluten-free often involves a bit of friendly experimentation. Keep notes on your process—the flour mix, water temperature, and rising time—so you can tweak the recipe to your kitchen's quirks. Each loaf will improve your skills and deepen your understanding.

Finally, don't forget the joy of sharing your homemade bread. Whether you make a sandwich for yourself or bring a fresh loaf to family and friends, this bread carries the satisfaction of making something nourishing with your own hands. No kneading, no stress—just simple ingredients, time, and care. Let the no-knead gluten-free sandwich loaf be your trusty baking companion on the road to becoming a confident, happy home baker.

Seeded Gluten-Free Artisan Boule

Baking an artisan boule without gluten can feel intimidating at first, but it's definitely achievable with the right approach and a little patience. This style of bread combines a rustic, crusty exterior with a soft, tender crumb, and when it's packed with seeds, it adds both flavor and texture that bring the loaf to life. The key here is to embrace the differences gluten-free baking demands rather than trying to force traditional methods onto the dough.

First off, selecting a balanced gluten-free flour blend is essential. Unlike wheat-based bread, which relies on gluten to provide structure and elasticity, gluten-free flours behave quite differently and usually need help from binding agents like xanthan gum, psyllium husk, or flaxseed meal. For our seeded artisan boule, a blend of rice flour, tapioca starch, and sorghum flour works beautifully. This trio offers a neutral base with a good balance of chewiness and lightness.

One aspect that can trip up new bakers is the dough consistency. Gluten-free doughs tend to be wetter and stickier than wheat dough, often more like a thick batter. That's perfectly normal. Trying to knead this dough as you would a traditional boule will only lead to frustration. Instead, use tools like a rubber spatula or a stand mixer fitted with a paddle attachment to combine your ingredients thoroughly. The goal is to hydrate all the flours evenly, so your seeds and other mix-ins distribute uniformly.

Incorporating seeds into your boule does more than just add crunch and flavor. Seeds contribute natural oils and nutrients that enrich the bread's texture and keep it moist longer. Sunflower, pumpkin, sesame, and flaxseeds are excellent choices here. Toasting the seeds lightly beforehand deepens their flavor and helps release their oils, making each bite more complex and satisfying. If you're including flaxseeds, it also doubles as a binding agent thanks to their mucilaginous quality.

Once you've mixed your dough and folded in the seeds, it needs to rest to allow the starches and binding agents to fully hydrate. This autolyse-like period is a game changer in gluten-free bread baking; it improves the dough's viscosity and results in a more elastic, easier-to-shape mass. About 30 to 45 minutes on the counter is usually enough. During this time, the dough will thicken, and you'll notice it becoming more manageable to work with, though still wet.

Shaping the boule is a totally different process here. You won't be able to shape gluten-free dough into a tight ball with the same springy feel of wheat dough. The trick is to use a well-floured surface—or better yet, parchment paper—and a gentle hand. Using wet or oiled hands, you can gather the dough into a loose round. Don't worry about perfection; the beauty of an artisan boule lies in its rustic imperfections. The loaf will hold its shape better by setting it seam-side down on a couche or parchment.

Proofing gluten-free dough is another step where patience pays off. Since these doughs lack gluten's spring, you won't see a dramatic rise like you do with wheat breads. Instead, look for subtle signs: a slight puffing, a smoother surface, and a bit more flexibility when poked lightly. Proof it in a warm, draft-free spot, loosely covered to prevent drying out. Around 60 to 90 minutes is typical, but that can vary depending on ambient temperature and yeast activity.

Baking this seeded gluten-free artisan boule is where the magic truly happens. To get a beautiful crust, preheat your oven to a high temperature, generally around 450°F (230°C), and bake the boule on a baking stone or steel if you have one. Adding steam during the first 15 minutes helps develop a glossy, crackly crust. You can create steam by placing a shallow pan of hot water in the oven or spraying water onto the oven walls right after putting the bread inside. This moisture delays crust setting and allows the loaf to expand fully.

The seeds on the exterior will toast beautifully during baking, giving the boule an inviting aroma and a pleasantly crunchy bite. Just before putting the dough in the oven, feel free to brush the top lightly with water or an egg wash if you're not restricted by dietary preferences—this can help seeds adhere better and promote crust color. For a vegan option, simply water works fine.

Gluten-free artisan boules can sometimes be gummy or dense if underbaked or if the hydration balance is off. One helpful trick is to bake the bread until it reaches an internal temperature of 205°F to 210°F (96°C to 99°C). Using a digital instant-read thermometer takes the guesswork out of timing, ensuring the crumb is fully cooked and has the perfect texture. After baking, let the boule cool completely on a wire rack to finish setting up. I know it's tempting to slice immediately, but patience here prevents a gummy interior.

Storing this seeded gluten-free boule requires some care. Gluten-free breads tend to dry out faster than traditional loaves, so wrapping your cooled bread in a clean kitchen towel and then placing it in a well-ventilated bread box or a paper bag keeps the crust crisp while maintaining moisture inside. For longer storage, slice and freeze the bread. You'll find that toasted slices from the freezer taste just as good as fresh.

Successfully baking a seeded gluten-free artisan boule not only yields a loaf with a crunchy crust and flavorful seeds but also boosts confidence in tackling gluten-free baking more broadly. This loaf can hold its own at any table, whether served alongside soups, salads, or your favorite spreads. As you practice, you'll learn how slight tweaks in flour ratios, hydration, and fermentation times influence the crumb and crust, turning you from a novice to a seasoned gluten-free baker.

So, don't be disheartened if your first attempts are a little sticky or oddly shaped. Every loaf is a learning experience, and with each bake, the process becomes more intuitive. Embrace the uniqueness of gluten-free bread – this boule is a perfect example of how flavor, texture, and rustic artisanal beauty can flourish even without gluten's presence.

Now that you've explored the essentials of a seeded gluten-free artisan boule, you're well on your way to expanding your baking repertoire. Remember, the heart of artisan bread baking lies as much in the journey as it does in the final crusty loaf sitting on your table. Happy baking!

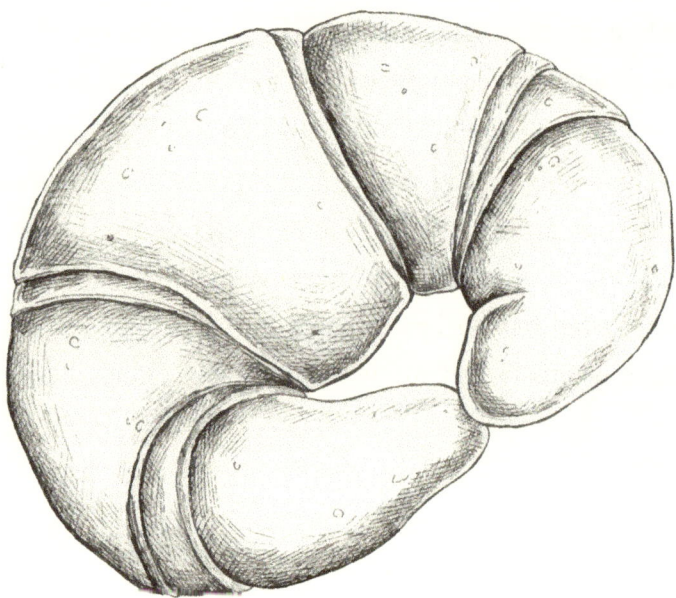

Chapter 10
Around-the-World Breads

---◆◆◆ ◆◆◆---

B read connects cultures in the most delicious ways, inviting home bakers to explore diverse traditions one loaf at a time. Venturing beyond familiar recipes opens up a world of textures, flavors, and techniques—from the crusty rolls warming tables in Mexico to the soft, pillowy loaves cherished in Japan. Each bread tells a story, shaped by history, local ingredients, and the care passed down through generations. This chapter encourages a joyful sense of discovery, showing that even beginner bakers can recreate these global staples with confidence. Embracing these international recipes sparks creativity while deepening your understanding of what bread truly means in kitchens everywhere—comfort, community, and craft all rolled into one. Whether you crave something sweet, savory, or hearty, this collection offers fun, approachable ways to expand your baking repertoire.

Mexican Bolillos and Conchas

Mexican bolillos and conchas are two iconic breads that hold a special place on bakery shelves and breakfast tables throughout Mexico. Both are deeply rooted in tradition, yet wonderfully approachable for the home baker eager to try something new and delicious. These loaves and rolls aren't just everyday breads; they carry stories of everyday life—from bustling street markets to quiet family mornings sipping coffee alongside freshly baked treats.

Starting with bolillos, these are the Mexico City version of a classic white roll, shaped into a small, crusty oval loaf. A bolillo's crust is thin but crisp, while its crumb is airy, tender, and slightly chewy. Traditionally, bolillos are baked very hot, often on a stone, to develop a beautiful golden crust that crackles just right. They're incredibly versatile—perfect for making tortas (Mexican sandwiches), accompanying soups, or simply eaten fresh with butter. For novice bakers, bolillos offer a great introduction to shaping techniques and creating bread with a delicate crust without being intimidating.

The preparation of bolillos leans heavily on the mastery of gluten development, which will give the loaf its elasticity and chewy texture. You'll want to handle the dough gently but with intention, practicing your kneading skills or even trying out stretch-and-fold methods covered earlier in this book. The classic bolillo dough uses simple ingredients: white bread flour, water, salt, sugar, and yeast. This simplicity allows you to focus on technique—especially the shaping step where the dough is rolled into a tight cylinder and then pinched down the middle before baking to give it that signature groove.

One of the challenges novices often face when baking bolillos is getting the crust just right. The secret lies in moisture and oven conditions. Bolillos need a steamy kick when they hit the oven, creating steam that helps form the thin, crisp exterior while the inside remains soft. Using a pan of water or spritzing the oven walls right after loading your rolls in can replicate those traditional bakery conditions at home. Don't be discouraged if your first attempt turns out softer than expected; this is a learning process, and your crust will steadily improve with each bake.

Moving on to conchas, these sweet breads are some of the most beloved in Mexican panaderías. What makes conchas stand out is their colorful, crunchy toppings that resemble seashells—hence their name, which means "shell" in Spanish. The bread itself is enriched, tender, and sweet, almost like a brioche but lighter to the touch. The magic really happens in the topping, which is a simple mixture of sugar, butter, and flour, sometimes flavored or colored with vanilla or cocoa powder. This topping cracks beautifully during baking, creating that iconic shell pattern that's as delightful to look at as it is to eat.

For anyone new to sweet breads, tackling conchas is a wonderfully rewarding project. Since the dough contains more fat and sugar than your average lean bread, it requires a slightly different approach to kneading and proofing, which are discussed in earlier chapters. Patience is key here—this enriched dough benefits from a longer rise to develop flavor and maintain softness. When shaping, the dough is portioned into rounds, then chilled before the topping is applied. This chilling step helps the topping adhere better and crack in the right way during baking.

One of the joys of baking conchas at home is experimenting with toppings. You're welcome to get creative beyond the classic vanilla and chocolate versions. Some bakers add food coloring to brighten their pan dulce, while others mix in spices like cinnamon or orange zest into the topping for a twist on tradition. This freedom to personalize makes baking conchas not just a cooking task but a creative activity that lifts your mood and connects you with Mexican culinary culture.

It's worth noting the importance of using the right flour for both bolillos and conchas, as this directly impacts texture and rise. Bread flour, with its higher protein content, is your best bet here. It builds enough gluten to give bolillos their characteristic chew and helps conchas rise well with their enriched, slightly heavier dough. If you remember the basics of gluten development from earlier chapters, you'll get a head start understanding how this impacts your results. On the other hand, avoiding too dense or heavy loaves means keeping an eye on fermentation times and not overloading the dough with fat or sugar, especially in conchas.

Both bolillos and conchas illustrate two wonderful points about bread baking: how simple ingredients can yield vastly different breads, and how shaping and topping techniques bring personality and flair. They are bread traditions that invite you to slow down a bit, enjoy the process, and savor something truly memorable. Learning to bake these breads builds confidence and adds exciting new options to your baking repertoire.

Another tip for perfecting these breads is to pay attention to room temperature and proofing environments. Since bolillos and conchas typically use commercial yeast, they respond well to warm rises between 75 and 80 degrees Fahrenheit. A cozy spot in your kitchen, like an oven with just the light on, can make all the difference in how the dough ferments and how the flavors develop. Don't rush these rises. Bread making is largely about time and patience, allowing natural fermentation to work its magic.

When it comes to storage, these breads are best enjoyed fresh. Bolillos maintain their optimal texture for about a day, so consider freezing any extras you won't consume quickly. Wrap them tightly and let them thaw at room temperature before reheating briefly in an oven. Conchas, given their delicate topping, should also be stored in an airtight container to keep the crust from becoming too soft. Usually, they're eaten within a day or two, fresh from the bakery or your oven, ideally with a cup of hot chocolate or coffee.

Finally, baking bolillos and conchas opens a window to understanding the broader cultural significance of bread in Mexican life. These breads connect generations, from street vendors selling them in the early morning to families sharing them at mealtime. They remind us that bread is more than food—it's a daily ritual, a comfort, and a way to nourish body and soul. For new bakers, making these breads at home isn't just about copying a recipe; it's participating in a long, delicious tradition.

Japanese Shokupan and Melonpan

When exploring breads from around the world, Japanese Shokupan and Melonpan stand out as fascinating examples of how tradition and creativity merge to form delicious everyday treats. Both are staples in Japan's bakery culture, but they offer very different textures and flavors that bring unique experiences to the table. Shokupan, often described as Japanese milk bread, is soft, pillowy, and slightly sweet, while Melonpan is a sweet bun with a crisp, cookie-like crust on top. Together, they represent a perfect introduction to Japanese-style breads, capturing the imagination of bakers looking for something both approachable and special.

Shokupan's signature characteristic is its incredibly tender crumb, which is airy yet substantial. What sets it apart from many Western sandwich breads is the use of a method called "Tangzhong," a water roux starter that involves cooking a portion of the flour and water (or milk) into a thick paste before mixing it with the rest of the dough ingredients. This technique helps the bread retain moisture longer, ensuring the loaf stays soft and fresh for days. For novice bakers, it's a neat trick to learn because it improves not just texture but also the bread's shelf life, making it ideal for everyday sandwiches or toast.

Melonpan tells a different story altogether. Its name directly translates to "melon bread," but interestingly, traditional Melonpan doesn't usually contain melon flavor.

Instead, the name comes from the bread's outer appearance, which resembles the rind of a melon, thanks to a grid pattern imprinted on the cookie-like crust. This crust is made by wrapping the soft yeast dough with a layer of sweet, crumbly cookie dough. When baked, it forms a contrast of textures: crunchy on the outside yet soft inside, creating a delightful bite. Some creative variations have incorporated melon or other flavors, but the classic relies purely on the marriage of these textures and its subtle sweetness to charm the eater.

Both Shokupan and Melonpan showcase Japan's talent for refining and adapting bread baking traditions to suit local tastes and preferences. While wheat bread was introduced relatively late to Japan's culinary heritage—only gaining popularity during the Meiji Restoration in the 19th century—the Japanese have since developed a style marked by exceptional softness and mild sweetness, quite distinct from the hearty European loaves or rustic sourdoughs you might have encountered before.

Making Shokupan at home is wonderfully rewarding and approachable even if you're new to bread baking. The dough starts with the usual suspects—flour, yeast, sugar, salt—but milk, butter, and sometimes eggs enrich it, producing that characteristic richness and chew. Rye flour or bread flour can be used depending on how much gluten development you want. Whichever flour you choose, expect a bit of kneading with the Tangzhong step in the background as your secret weapon for success. The dough is usually proofed in a square or rectangular loaf pan, resulting in the classic "pull-apart" slices that are perfect for sandwiches or breakfast toast piled high with butter or jam.

One of the challenges home bakers might face when tackling Shokupan is recognizing when the dough has proofed enough. Because of its softness, it can go from perfectly risen to over-proofed very quickly if left unattended. Your hands-on observation—checking for springiness and gentle poke tests—will become reliable over time. Additionally, the oven baking environment plays a major role. A well-heated oven with a bit of steam can help develop a soft, slightly shiny crust rather than a hard, cracked surface you might expect from European-style breads.

Melonpan, on the other hand, challenges you to balance two different dough components: the airy yeast bread and the sweet cookie dough crust. The cookie dough is usually made with butter, sugar, flour, and egg—simple ingredients, but their proportions have to be just right to avoid spreading too much during baking. If the cookie dough spreads too thin, it won't have that signature crisp texture or the charming ridged pattern on top. To help retain the shape and contrast, some bakers chill the dough before assembly and carefully score the top with a knife to create the classic grid lines.

While it may feel intimidating at first to combine two types of dough, Melonpan is surprisingly forgiving once you understand the layering process. Start by rolling out the cookie dough into a flat disk and wrapping it carefully over the proofed yeast dough ball. Making sure the cookie layer doesn't tear or break is key—it's what maintains the structural integrity and original look. During baking, the contrast between the crunchy cookie layer and soft bread beneath wins applause from everyone who tries it.

Both breads present wonderful opportunities to customize flavors as well. Shokupan can be enriched with hints of matcha powder, cocoa, or even sweet potato puree, bringing gentle new notes without overpowering its signature mildness. Melonpan invites toppings like a light dusting of powdered sugar, cocoa for a chocolate crust, or even fillings such as custard or red bean paste, inspired by Japanese dessert traditions. These variations can add another layer of excitement for budding bakers wanting to experiment beyond the classic forms.

From a practical standpoint, these breads highlight important skills every beginner baker should appreciate. Shokupan teaches you to be patient with the fermentation process and gentle with handling delicate dough, while Melonpan encourages precision layering and combining two dough textures in harmony. Both strengthen your grasp of proofing, shaping, and baking temperature control.

In terms of serving and enjoying, Shokupan is often enjoyed toasted, with toppings ranging from simple butter and jam to savory spreads or eggs for breakfast or light lunches. Its tenderness makes even simple sandwiches feel special. Meanwhile, Melonpan is often sold as a grab-and-go treat at Japanese bakeries or convenience stores, enjoyed as a snack or dessert with coffee or tea. Its sweet crunch is notoriously addictive, and baking it yourself ensures fresh, warm bites that are hard to resist.

In summary, Japanese Shokupan and Melonpan open a delightful door into Japanese bread baking that is well worth exploring. They highlight techniques that support softness and moisture retention, but also invite playful textures and sweetness. As you practice making these breads, you'll find your confidence grow. Both breads prove that with just a few ingredients and thoughtful technique, you can create loaves and buns that feel both elegant and everyday at once.

So take your time with the Tangzhong method for Shokupan and the layering skill needed for Melonpan. Enjoy the process as much as the delicious results. Before long, your kitchen will smell like a cozy Japanese bakery, and you might discover these breads becoming staples in your homemade bread repertoire.

Middle-Eastern Manakish and Za'atar Bread

Continuing our global bread journey, let's explore the vibrant flavors and traditions of Middle-Eastern manakish and za'atar bread. These breads are wonderfully simple yet deeply rooted in centuries of culinary heritage. Manakish, sometimes known as the Middle Eastern pizza, is a round, flat bread generously topped with za'atar, a fragrant blend of herbs, sumac, and sesame seeds. This bread is beloved for breakfast, snacks, or even light meals, and it's remarkably easy to make for beginners eager to add some exotic flair to their baking repertoire.

At its core, manakish is a lean dough, usually made with basic ingredients: flour, water, a pinch of salt, yeast, and a touch of olive oil. The dough offers a soft, pillowy base with just enough chew to hold the flavorful za'atar topping without becoming soggy. Because the dough is relatively straightforward, it's a great practice in handling yeast-based breads that don't require intensive kneading or long fermentation times. You'll soon realize how adaptable and forgiving this dough can be – ideal qualities when you're building up confidence at the mixing bowl.

Za'atar itself is what sets these breads apart. It's a mix of dried thyme, oregano, marjoram, toasted sesame seeds, sumac, and salt, creating a wonderfully aromatic and tangy seasoning. While za'atar blends differ by region and family recipes, the common elements bring a burst of herbal and nutty flavors that pair beautifully with the olive oil used both in the dough and brushed on top before baking. If you can't find premade za'atar, making your own mix at home is surprisingly easy and rewarding. Toasting sesame seeds and grinding fresh dried herbs can elevate the dish and introduce you to the satisfying side of spice blending.

Speaking of olive oil, it's an essential character in this bread's story. High-quality extra virgin olive oil not only moistens the dough but also enriches the flavor and helps achieve a golden, crisp exterior during baking. When spreading za'atar over the dough, mixing it with olive oil creates a paste that clings beautifully to the surface instead of falling off or burning. This step might seem simple, but it's key to the hallmark taste and texture of manakish.

As you prepare the dough, pay attention to hydration. Middle Eastern flatbreads, including manakish, generally have moderate hydration levels—too wet, and the dough becomes hard to shape; too dry, and you lose that tender crumb under the za'atar topping. The goal is a smooth, elastic dough that's easy to roll or stretch out into circles about 6 to 8 inches in diameter. Feel free to experiment with thickness—some prefer a thinner crust for crispness, while others like it thicker for a chewier bite. Either way, the dough should not be overly thick, as it can interfere with the balance between bread and za'atar.

After shaping, the dough proofs quickly—often just 30 to 45 minutes at warm room temperature is enough for a gentle rise. This short proof suits quick meals, which is why manakish is a popular street food across Lebanon, Syria, Jordan, and Palestine. The faster turnaround can be quite exciting for home bakers still wrestling with lengthy dough fermentations. No long waiting times means you can satisfy your baking cravings in just a couple of hours from start to finish.

Baking manakish requires a hot oven to deliver a crisp, golden crust and well-cooked topping. Typically, temperatures between 475°F and 500°F (245°C to 260°C) work best. If you have a pizza stone, preheat it thoroughly—it simulates the traditional stone ovens used in Middle Eastern bakeries, providing even heat and a beautifully blistered bottom crust. Without a stone, a sturdy baking sheet turned upside down can help mimic this effect. Manakish bakes quickly—five to eight minutes usually does the trick. Keep an eye on your first batch to gauge the perfect timing for your oven setup.

Beyond the classic za'atar topping, manakish recipes often include variations featuring cheese, ground meat, or spinach. However, for beginners, starting with za'atar keeps the process simple and celebrates the bread's cultural essence. The herbaceous, slightly tangy taste of za'atar with the golden crust is a crowd-pleaser, even for those unfamiliar with Middle Eastern flavors. Pair your fresh manakish with labneh, fresh tomatoes, olives, or a drizzle of tahini, and you have a feeding frenzy for any meal of the day.

Mastering manakish also opens doors to exploring broader Middle Eastern bread traditions. Za'atar bread, in particular, is sometimes made as a flatbread without any yeast—a simple dough of flour, water, olive oil, salt, and the za'atar mixture pressed into the surface. This unleavened version bakes quickly and results in a more cracker-like texture, perfect for snacking or dipping.

It's important to embrace the rustic nature of manakish dough during baking. Small imperfections in shape or slight bubbles on the surface add charm and authenticity, rather than detract from it. As you grow more comfortable, you'll notice how easy it is to play with the dough's elasticity and how the dough responds to different handling techniques. Don't be discouraged if your first attempts don't look perfectly round or evenly topped; practice and patience make a tremendous difference with these flatbreads.

Another useful tip involves the way za'atar is spread. Instead of simply sprinkling it on, mix the za'atar with olive oil to create a paste with the right spreadability and to protect the herbs from burning too quickly in the oven. Applying this paste evenly prevents dry spots and ensures every bite includes the vibrant flavors that make this bread special. Some bakers even swirl the za'atar mixture into the dough's surface gently with their fingertips for an inviting marbled effect.

Once baked, manakish is best enjoyed fresh and warm. The aroma that fills your kitchen as it bakes is unforgettable— earthy herbs, nutty sesame, and that unmistakable tang from sumac. For serving, warm manakish can be torn into pieces and shared, often with simple accompaniments like cucumbers, mint, or a drizzle of olive oil. Leftovers can be reheated briefly in a hot oven or toaster oven to revive crispness, though best not to store too long to preserve the vibrant flavors.

Adopting manakish and za'atar bread into your baking routine can expand your palate and your skills. It's a brilliant way to experiment with herb blends and olive oil quality, learn the ropes with lean dough handling, and incorporate fast-rising, high-heat baking into your kitchen. You'll find this bread fills an everyday niche while inviting moments of exploration and cultural appreciation with every bite. Start with the basics and let your curiosity guide you to variations that suit your taste and schedule.

In the spectrum of global breads, Middle Eastern manakish and za'atar bread sit comfortably between humble ingredients and rich heritage. They honor centuries of shared meals while inviting modern bakers like you to participate in a timeless tradition. Don't worry about perfection here; focus on the sensory pleasure—the smell, the texture, the bright flavors—and the joy of sharing something homemade. You'll soon discover how approachable and rewarding flatbread baking can be with just a few pantry staples and a bit of patience.

Nordic Rugbrød and Knækbrød

Moving into the world of Nordic breads, two staples stand out for home bakers interested in exploring hearty, traditional flavors: Rugbrød and Knækbrød. Both types hold a special place in Scandinavian cuisine and are excellent additions to your baking repertoire. They offer unique textures and flavors that celebrate simplicity, whole grains, and often, sourdough techniques, making them approachable for beginners yet rewarding to master.

Rugbrød, often called Danish rye bread, is a dense, dark loaf made primarily from rye flour. Unlike lighter wheat breads, it's robust and slightly sour, resulting from long fermentation times that deepen the flavors. At first glance, its dense crumb might feel intimidating, but don't let that fool you. Rugbrød's richness and tang come from a blend of rye flour, sometimes mixed with whole rye berries or cracked grains, coupled with a sourdough starter or a slow yeast fermentation. These elements give the bread its chew and its characteristic moist texture.

What makes Rugbrød particularly special is how it embraces whole grains and natural fermentation, which together create a bread that's incredibly nutritious and satisfying. Rye itself contains less gluten than wheat, which means you won't get that airy, fluffy texture typical of wheat breads. Instead, expect a tight crumb and a slightly sticky interior that's perfect for hearty sandwiches, especially topped with traditional Danish toppings like pickled herring, liver pate, or creamy cheese.

Getting started with Rugbrød requires attention to a few key factors. The flour mix is essential — rye flour behaves very differently from wheat flour. It absorbs more water and forms less gluten, so your dough will be wetter and stickier. This can be surprising if you're used to shaping firm, elastic wheat doughs. Instead of kneading like normal, you often rely on longer fermentation and mixing techniques to develop the dough's structure.

Because rye flour has little gluten, it's impossible to develop the stretch and elasticity that wheat bread offers. This means that shaping the loaf is a gentler process — you want to handle the dough lightly to retain its gas bubbles without punch-downs or heavy kneading. Many traditional Rugbrød recipes use a loaf pan to help it maintain shape during baking. You'll find that the crust darkens beautifully, often accented with sunflower seeds, whole rye grains, or even oats pressed on top for extra texture and visual appeal.

One motivational aspect of Rugbrød is its longevity. Thanks to rye's natural components and the dense crumb, this bread keeps well without drying out quickly. It actually improves in flavor a day or two after baking, making it ideal for bakers who love to plan ahead. For storing, simply wrap in a clean kitchen towel or place in a bread bag, and it will remain moist and inviting, perfect for slicing and enjoying slowly over breakfasts or lunches.

Knækbrød, by contrast, is a crispbread, a traditional Nordic cracker made mainly from rye flour. Its name literally means "crack bread," referring to the satisfying crunch it delivers. It's thinner, crispier, and perfect as a snack or accompaniment to soft cheeses, spreads, or smoked fish. While Rugbrød is dense and moist, Knækbrød is the ideal companion when you're in the mood for something lighter and crunchier but still with that hearty rye flavor.

What makes Knækbrød accessible is its relatively simple dough and baking method. It typically combines rye flour with water, salt, and sometimes a bit of oil or honey for flavor balance. Seeds such as sesame, flax, sunflower, or caraway are frequent additions, lending both crunch and subtle bursts of flavor. The dough is rolled very thin, docked or cut into shapes, and baked slowly until golden and crisp.

For novice bakers, Knækbrød offers a low-stress project with great results. Because the dough isn't leavened and doesn't need rising time, you can mix and bake it straight away — an instant win if you want something flavorful without intensive hands-on work. Its crisp texture also means it stores exceptionally well, staying crunchy for weeks if kept in an airtight container.

Baking Knækbrød provides an opportunity to experiment with seeds and spices. Adding fennel or caraway seeds infuses the crackers with a pleasant aroma that's very traditional. Plus, they're naturally gluten-aware as many recipes focus on rye, which some people find easier to digest. Since the dough is more of a batter or very sticky, rolling it thin can be a bit tricky, but using parchment paper or a silicone mat helps avoid sticking and makes transferring easier.

When baking Nordic breads like Rugbrød and Knækbrød, temperature and timing are crucial. Rugbrød benefits from a long bake at a moderate temperature to develop its characteristic chewy crust without drying out the interior. Pressure is off regarding wild bubbles and oven spring, but patience pays off with a complex aroma and satisfying bite. Knækbrød, on the other hand, requires lower heat for longer to fully dry out and crisp the crackers without burning the sugars or seeds.

Historically, these breads have been a cornerstone of Nordic sustenance, prized for their ability to nourish through long winters and active days. Rugbrød especially is emblematic of Scandinavian frugality and respect for natural ingredients, while Knækbrød represents practicality in portability and shelf life. Incorporating them into your baking practice not only gives you authentic tastes and textures but also connects you to a tradition of wholesome, honest food.

For first-timers, it might be tempting to try to make a lighter, wheat-like rye bread, but embracing the differences rye brings makes for a more successful loaf. Watching the dough's unique behavior, feeling that wet, sticky rye dough, and learning to trust slow fermentation can feel like a breakthrough. These skills build a strong foundation for all kinds of rustic, whole-grain loaves and shift your baker's intuition toward grain-friendly techniques.

Serving suggestions for Rugbrød often reflect its dense, hearty nature. Think open-faced sandwiches topped with smoked salmon, creamy spreads, pickled vegetables, or sharp cheeses. It's a staple with butter and a slice of cheese as much as with elaborate seafood toppings. Knækbrød shines with soft cheeses, smears of butter and honey, or simply dipped in soups and stews for a crunchy contrast. Both breads, through their textures and flavors, invite slower eating and appreciation, which is something many home bakers find deeply satisfying.

In terms of ingredients, sourcing good-quality rye flour makes a big difference. Look for stone-ground or whole rye for the richest flavor. Store-bought rye flour often varies in freshness, so keeping it in a cool spot or the fridge helps maintain its taste and prevent spoilage. Seeds can be toasted lightly beforehand to heighten aroma for Knækbrød, and experimenting with different seed proportions can personalize your crackers.

Ultimately, the joy of Nordic bread baking lies in its simplicity paired with thoughtful patience. These breads may not rise like fluffy sandwich loaves, but the attention to fermentation rhythms, grain details, and baking time rewards you with truly unique breads. They have a soulfulness and nourishment that's perfect for home bakers looking to expand beyond familiar breads and add global inspirations to their kitchen.

Whether you start with the dense and tangy Rugbrød or the crispy, seed-studded Knækbrød, you'll discover that Nordic breads offer a rewarding experience. Each bite tells a story rooted in centuries of tradition and a respect for humble ingredients transformed through time and technique. These breads are proof that mastering bread baking is as much about listening and adapting to each flour and dough as it is about following recipes.

Conclusion

Bread baking is more than just following a recipe—it's an embrace of patience, a dance with time, and a celebration of simple ingredients transformed into something truly special. Throughout this book, the journey from flour and water to a golden loaf has unfolded step-by-step with care and clarity. For those who started with little more than curiosity and a kitchen, the progress made here is nothing short of remarkable. This final section is a reflection on that journey and an encouragement to keep expanding your love of baking.

The real magic behind bread baking happens in small moments and subtle adjustments. Perhaps it was the first time you noticed how flour hydration feels in your hands or how bubbles forming during fermentation signal that the yeast is alive and kicking. These are the building blocks of intuition, the kind of knowledge no recipe can fully capture. As you grow more comfortable with these subtle cues, your bread will improve naturally—not because you slavishly follow instructions, but because you're learning to listen and respond to your dough.

Don't be discouraged by early imperfections. Every baker, no matter how experienced, encounters collapsed loaves, dense crumb, or underwhelming crusts. These are not signs of failure but stepping stones toward mastery. Mistakes are a baker's best teachers. When a loaf doesn't rise as expected or tastes less than perfect, it's worth asking yourself what might be different this time. Was the yeast fresh? Was the dough properly hydrated? Did the room temperature change? These questions guide trial, discovery, and ultimately, success.

The treasures of bread baking also come from the versatility it offers. Think about all the breads you can make—from no-knead overnight loaves perfect for busy mornings to the intricate, buttery richness of a brioche. Each variety teaches you different techniques and flavors, broadening your skill set. You've seen how quick breads work well for convenience, artisan loaves add elegance, and even gluten-free options cater to diverse needs—all while keeping the process approachable and rewarding.

One of the greatest joys of bread baking is sharing. There's something deeply human about breaking fresh bread with others, whether at a holiday meal or a casual family dinner. The aroma wafting from your oven brings everybody to the kitchen, and the smiles that follow the first bite are the ultimate reward. Over time, these moments become memorable family traditions. Bread becomes not just nourishment but a symbol of care, connection, and home.

While this book provides the foundation, tools, and inspiration, your own kitchen adventures will add layers to what you've learned here. Experiment with different flours, hydration levels, or fermentation times. Try shaping your loaves in new ways or infusing them with herbs, seeds, or dried fruits. The beauty of bread baking lies in its endless adaptability—you're never truly done learning or perfecting your craft.

It's also important to remember that baking bread is a way to slow down and find calm. In a world that often rushes forward at a dizzying pace, kneading dough and watching it transform offers a moment of mindfulness. You're fully present, engaged with your hands and senses in a creative rhythm. This simple act nurtures not only delicious bread but a sense of peace and accomplishment.

Every baker's path is unique, influenced by personal tastes, kitchen setups, and even climate. Don't hesitate to adjust techniques or timing to suit your environment. What's most important is to enjoy the process, celebrate progress, and remain curious. Sometimes the best loaves come from daring to stray from the rules just a little and making the recipe your own.

As you continue exploring bread baking, you may find that it touches other areas of your life. It teaches patience, resilience, and the virtues of slow work. It can spark creativity in the kitchen, inviting you to pair your breads with homemade jams, artisan cheeses, or hearty soups. In this way, bread is not just food—it becomes a springboard for a richer culinary life and deeper connections.

It's easy to get caught up in results, especially with baking where precision matters. But don't forget to savor the experience itself. Each batch, whether triumphant or flawed, is a moment of learning and self-expression. Over time, you'll gain confidence and the knowledge to troubleshoot instinctively. The skills and intuition you acquire will make what once seemed intimidating feel natural and joyful.

Going forward, keep bread baking fun and approachable. Share your successes and even your mishaps with friends or baking communities. There's a warmth in knowing others share your passion and challenges. This camaraderie can spur new ideas and deepen your connection to the craft.

In sum, this book has been an invitation—to learn the essential techniques, to explore the diverse world of breads, and to develop your own baking voice. Whether you stick to classic loaves or venture into artisan and international recipes, the satisfaction of turning simple ingredients into something nourishing and beautiful remains at the heart of it all. Don't underestimate how satisfying it is to pull a loaf fresh from the oven, its crust crackling under your touch and its crumb soft yet structured. That feeling is the reward of persistence, curiosity, and a few humble ingredients coming together.

So, as you close this chapter and look toward more baking adventures, remember: every loaf matters. Every loaf is a step forward, an act of creation, and a testament to your newfound skills and patience. Keep your kitchen warm, your flour close, and your spirit curious. The world of bread is rich and welcoming, ready to reward your efforts with loaves that nourish both body and soul.

Appendix

Baking bread at home is a journey filled with learning, experimentation, and a fair share of delightful surprises. This appendix is here to offer you extra support—a handy toolbox of tips, quick references, and reminders that can make your bread-baking experience smoother and more enjoyable. Think of it as a friendly companion for those moments when you need just a bit more guidance or a quick refresher.

Inside, you'll find useful conversion charts, glossaries of common baking terms, and handy troubleshooting checklists. These resources save you from having to flip back through earlier chapters or waste time searching for answers. Whether it's understanding measurement substitutions or recalling the ideal proofing times, this section aims to keep things straightforward and accessible.

Also included are best practices for storing your bread to keep it fresh longer, along with tips on freezing and thawing without losing that just-baked flavor and texture you worked so hard to achieve. Because nothing's more disappointing than letting a beautiful loaf go to waste.

Don't hesitate to return here whenever you feel stuck or just want a quick bit of inspiration. Remember, every baker—no matter how experienced—refers back to trusted notes and tips now and then. Mastery comes one loaf at a time, with patience and practice as your best ingredients.

Happy baking, and may your kitchen always smell like fresh bread!

www.ingramcontent.com/pod-product-compliance
Lightning Source LLC
Chambersburg PA
CBHW021225090426
42740CB00006B/380